impact

3A

SERIES EDITORS
JoAnn (Jodi) Crandall
Joan Kang Shin

AUTHOR
Diane Pinkley

NATIONAL
GEOGRAPHIC
LEARNING | CENGAGE
Learning·

Australia • Brazil • Mexico • Singapore • United Kingdom • United States

Thank you to the educators who provided invaluable feedback during the development of *Impact*:

EXPERT PANEL

Márcia Ferreira, Academic Coordinator, CCBEU, Franca, Brazil

Jianwei Song, Vice-general Manager, Ensure International Education, Harbin, China

María Eugenia Flores, Academic Director, and **Liana Rojas-Binda**, Head of Recruitment & Training, Centro Cultural Costarricense-Norteamericano, San José, Costa Rica

Liani Setiawati, M.Pd., SMPK 1 BPK PENABUR Bandung, Bandung, Indonesia

Micaela Fernandes, Head of Research and Development Committee and Assessment Committee, Pui Ching Middle School, Macau

Héctor Sánchez Lozano, Academic Director, and **Carolina Tripodi**, Head of the Juniors Program, Proulex, Guadalajara, Mexico

Rosario Giraldez, Academic Director, Alianza Cultural, Montevideo, Uruguay

REVIEWERS

BRAZIL

Renata Cardoso, Colégio do Sol, Guara, DF

Fábio Delano Vidal Carneiro, Colégio Sete de Setembro, Fortaleza

Cristiano Carvalho, Centro Educacional Leonardo da Vinci, Vitória

Silvia Corrêa, Associação Alumni, São Paulo

Carol Espinosa, Associação Cultural Brasil Estados Unidos, Salvador

Marcia Ferreira, Centro Cultural Brasil Estados Unidos, Franca

Clara Haddad, ELT Consultant, São Paulo

Elaine Carvalho Chaves Hodgson, Colégio Militar de Brasília, Brasília

Thays Farias Galvão Ladosky, Associação Brasil América, Recife

Itana Lins, Colégio Anchieta, Salvador

Samantha Mascarenhas, Associação Cultural Brasil Estados Unidos, Salvador

Ann Marie Moreira, Pan American School of Bahia, Bahia

Rodrigo Ramirez, CEETEPS- Fatec Zona Sul, São Paulo

Paulo Torres, Vitória Municipality, Vitória

Renata Zainotte, Go Up Idiomas, Rio de Janeiro

CHINA

Zhou Chao, MaxEn Education, Beijing

Zhu Haojun, Only International Education, Shanghai

Su Jing, Beijing Chengxun International English School, Beijing

Jianjun Shen, Phoenix City International School, Guangzhou

COSTA RICA

Luis Antonio Quesada-Umaña, Centro Cultural Costarricense Norteamericano, San José

INDONESIA

Luz S. Ismail, M.A., LIA Institute of Language and Vocational Training, Jakarta

Selestin Zainuddin, LIA Institute of Language and Vocational Training, Jakarta

Rosalia Dian Devitasari, SMP Kolese Kanisius, Jakarta

JAPAN

John Williams, Tezukayama Gakuen, Nara

MEXICO

Nefertiti González, Instituto Mexicano Madero, Puebla

Eugenia Islas, Instituto Tlalpan, Mexico City

Marta MM Seguí, Colegio Velmont A.C., Puebla

SOUTH KOREA

Min Yuol (Alvin) Cho, Global Leader English Education, Yong In

THAILAND

Panitnan Kalayanapong, Eduzone Co., Ltd., Bangkok

TURKEY

Damla Çaltuğ, İELEV, Istanbul

Basak Nalcakar Demiralp, Ankara Sinav College, Ankara

Humeyra Olcayli, İstanbul Bilim College, Istanbul

VIETNAM

Chantal Kruger, ILA Vietnam, Hô Chí Minh

Ai Nguyen Huynh, Vietnam USA Society, Hô Chí Minh

impact

3A

Scope and Sequence

	1 **Who Am I?** page 8	**2** **Misunderstood Animals** page 24	**3** **Everybody's Doing It!** page 42	**4** **Fashion Footprints** page 58
THEME	Teen identity and personality	Animals in popular culture	Human and animal group behaviour	Making responsible fashion choices
VOCABULARY STRATEGY	· Suffix -ous · Using context	· Prefixes mis- and un- · Using a thesaurus	· Synonyms · Definitions and examples	· Suffix -al · Using a dictionary
SPEAKING STRATEGY	Comparing and contrasting	Expressing surprise and disbelief	Expressing cause and effect	Asking for clarification and clarifying
GRAMMAR	**Question tags:** Confirming information or seeking agreement *Alicia is friendly, isn't she?* **Special uses of *it*:** *I hate it when the alarm goes off.*	**Modals:** Speculating about the past *He refuses to go in the water. He might have seen a jellyfish.* **Infinitives with and without *to*:** *He doesn't want to hold rats. Make him try it.*	**Separable and inseparable two-word verbs:** *They worked out a solution.* ***Enough, too many, too much*:** Talking about amounts: *I have enough pillows, but there are not enough feathers. I need more.*	**Present passive:** Describing actions and processes *A lot of pesticides are used to grow cotton.* **Modals:** Making suggestions and giving advice about present and past actions *You shouldn't have bought that leather jacket.*
READING	*Why Am I Me?*	*Vampire Bats – The Truth Exposed!*	*Humans in Groups*	*A Passion for Fashion*
READING STRATEGY	Identify descriptive words	Distinguish supporting details	Look for definitions and examples	Compare and contrast
VIDEO	*What Makes Up an Identity?*	*Face-to-Face with a Leopard Seal*	*Smarter by the Swarm*	*How Your T-Shirt Can Make a Difference*
MISSION	**Be Determined** National Geographic Explorer: **Jack Andraka**, Inventor	**Keep an Open Mind** National Geographic Explorer: **Jenny Daltry**, Herpetologist and Conservationist	**Collaborate** National Geographic Explorer: **Iain Couzin**, Behavioural Ecologist	**Make Good Choices** National Geographic Explorer: **Asher Jay**, Creative Conservationist
WRITING	Genre: **Comparison and contrast essay** Focus: Compare and contrast	Genre: **Process description** Focus: Describe purpose and sequence	Genre: **Exemplification essay** Focus: Give examples	Genre: **Persuasive essay** Focus: Introduce facts and opinion
PRONUNCIATION	Intonation in question tags	Modals + *have* + past participle	Pausing	*Shouldn't have* + past participle
EXPRESS YOURSELF	Creative Expression: **Flash fiction** *A Day in the Life* Making connections: Teen identity and misunderstood animals		Creative Expression: **Poem** *The Garb Age* Making connections: Fashion trends and group behaviour	

Unit 1

JACK ANDRAKA Inventor

When Jack Andraka was 15 years old, he invented a test to detect certain types of cancer. Jack hopes he can inspire other young people to pursue their passions. He believes that everyone has the power to make a difference. What are you passionate about?

Unit 2

JENNY DALTRY Herpetologist and Conservationist

Jenny Daltry has always loved reptiles. She collected lizards, frogs and snakes near her home when she was a child. She also volunteered at a zoo. When Jenny was 18, she travelled to India to work on a crocodile farm. There she realised she wanted to become a herpetologist: someone who studies reptiles.

Unit 3

IAIN COUZIN Behavioural Ecologist

Iain Couzin uses maths to study how animals behave in groups. With mathematical models, he can take a closer look at bird migrations, insect colonies and schools of fish. Iain thinks we can use this research to answer questions about our world, such as 'How do animals benefit from working in groups?' and 'Can humans learn from animal behaviour to work better in groups?'

Unit 4

ASHER JAY Creative Conservationist

Do you think about where your clothes come from? Asher Jay does! She paints, writes and designs fashions that help raise awareness for sustainability and conservation. Asher feels very connected to the environment and to all living things, even plants and bugs. That's why she wants to reduce her fashion footprint and inspire others to do the same.

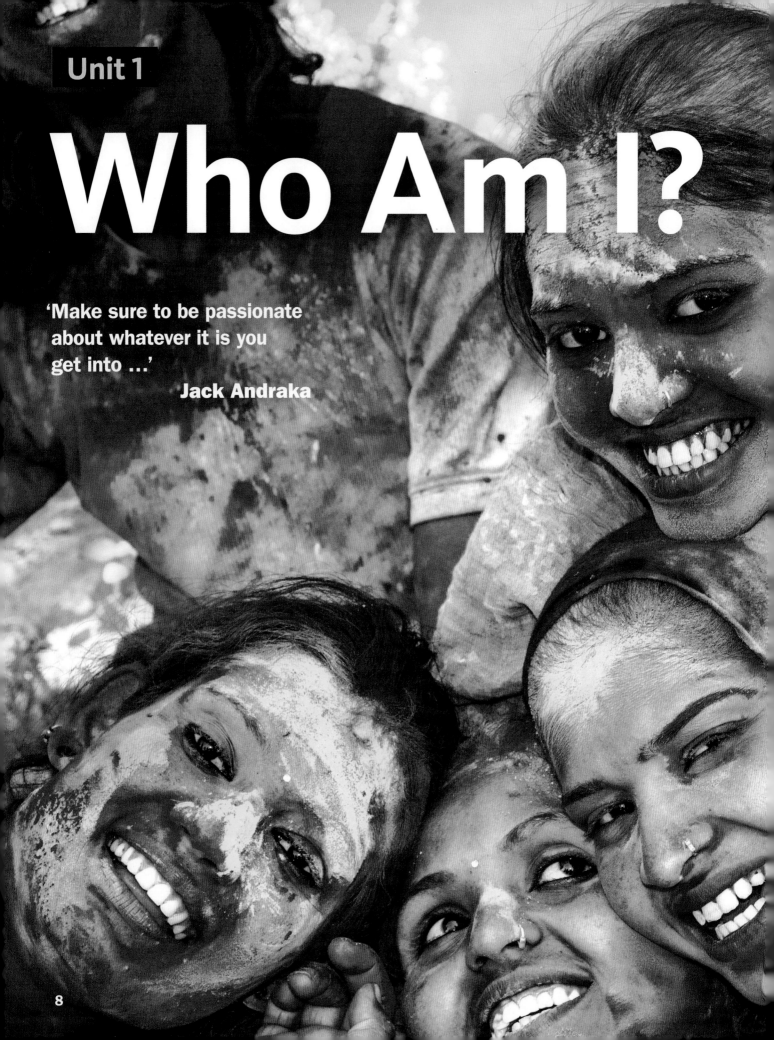

Who Am I?

'Make sure to be passionate about whatever it is you get into …'

Jack Andraka

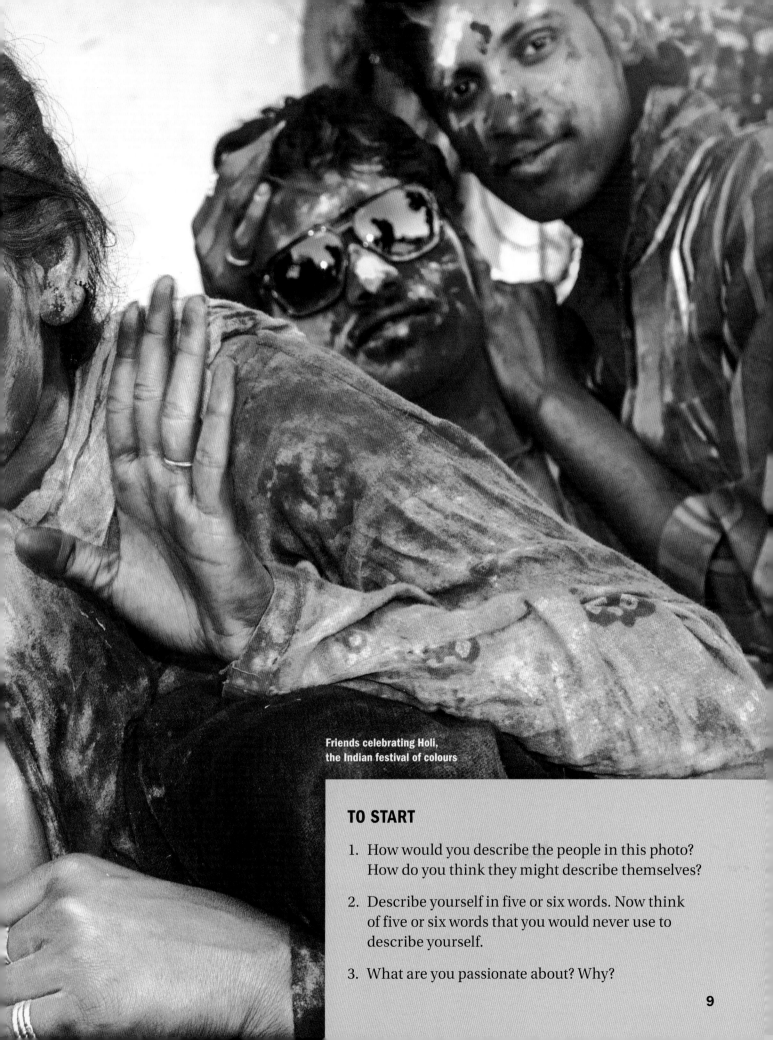

Friends celebrating Holi,
the Indian festival of colours

TO START

1. How would you describe the people in this photo? How do you think they might describe themselves?

2. Describe yourself in five or six words. Now think of five or six words that you would never use to describe yourself.

3. What are you passionate about? Why?

9

For teenagers, life can seem exciting and confusing at the same time, can't it? As a teenager, you're on your way to becoming an adult. It's a time of important changes and important questions.

A lot of these questions are about **identity**, or who you are. You're an individual, but you're also a product of your family life, your social environment and your culture. Your identity includes your beliefs, your values and your actions. You learnt your values from your family, but, as a teenager, you may become less interested in what your family thinks. You may choose to spend more time with other people whose values and personalities are like yours. That's natural.

Then there's **personality**, or the qualities that make you different from other people. If you love parties and are **enthusiastic** about meeting lots of new people, you're probably **outgoing** and **self-confident**. If you get excellent marks at school, chances are you're **organised** and **responsible**. If you're **energetic** or adventurous, you might like hiking, or getting together with friends to explore a cave! If you're **optimistic**, **generous** and **patient**, you might enjoy helping by spending time with animals at a shelter, or by participating in a local clean-up event.

Personality is tricky. You might assume that everyone sees you the way you see yourself, but that isn't always true. Friends may laugh at your stories and think you have a great **sense of humour**, but your brother might think you're just odd. You may see yourself as **ambitious** because you're **determined** to get what you want, but others may feel you're stubborn, or unwilling to take advice. You may feel self-conscious and **shy**, while other people may think you're unfriendly. You may think you're fair, but you may still seem unreasonable or unkind to a friend.

Understanding yourself and how others see you can really be a puzzle!

2 **LEARN NEW WORDS Listen and repeat.** 🎧 003

3 **Work in pairs.** Make another list of five or six words that describe you, using the new vocabulary. Then make a list of five or six words that describe your partner. Compare your lists. Do you agree with your partner's description of you? Why or why not?

4 **Read and write the words from the list.**

ambitious	determined	enthusiastic	generous
optimistic	organised	outgoing	self-confident

By the time Jack Andraka was 14 years old, he was very _____ about science. Jack really wanted to focus on cancer research. He came up with a cheap, fast way to detect a type of cancer. When he first proposed his idea, some adults thought that Jack was being too _____ , but he was _____ to prove them wrong. He stayed _____ and entered his idea into an international science fair. Jack won! Now he feels more _____ . People have even asked him to be on TV because of his _____ personality and creative ideas.

5 **LEARN NEW WORDS Listen to the words.** Write each trait next to the correct example. Are these words positive or negative? Decide. Then listen and repeat. 🎧004 005

2014 Emerging Explorer, inventor Jack Andraka

fair	odd	self-conscious	stubborn

_____ 1. You never change! Just listen to me for once.

_____ 2. You put salt and pepper on your ice cream? Wow!

_____ 3. I like our music teacher. In her class, everyone gets a chance to play.

_____ 4. Oh, come on. Nobody is looking at you. Let's dance.

6 **YOU DECIDE Choose an activity. Work in pairs.**

1. Together, think of a famous person, such as a singer, actor or internet personality. Separately, list as many descriptive words as you can about that person. Are any of your words the same? Do you agree with your partner's description?

2. As a student, you're an expert on teachers. Think about teachers you've had and write words to describe them. Look at the positive qualities you both listed. Then work together to write a description of your ideal teacher.

3. Write the letters in your partner's name down the side of a piece of paper. Then write a word that describes your partner for each letter. When you've finished, compare your name poems. Do you agree with your partner's description?

Musical
Ambitious
Responsible
Curious
Organised

Comparing	Contrasting
You're <u>outgoing</u>? So am I!	You're <u>shy</u>? Not me! I'm not <u>shy</u> at all.
Just like you, I'm <u>self-confident</u>.	Unlike you, I'm <u>optimistic</u>.
We're alike because we're both <u>patient</u>.	I'm <u>determined</u>, but you're just <u>stubborn</u>!

1 **Listen.** How do the speakers compare and contrast their younger brothers? Write the words and phrases you hear. ⚲007

2 **Read and complete the dialogue.**

Dave: My aunt and uncle are visiting this week.

Nina: You don't seem very happy about it.

Dave: I'm not. My aunt is always saying, 'You're _____ your uncle Jack!'

Nina: Well, are you and your uncle _____ ?

Dave: No, we're very different. _____ him, I'm active and outgoing. All he does is watch TV.

Nina: Is he funny? Optimistic? Generous, _____ you?

Dave: No way. _____ ! He never gives me anything, not even on my birthday.

3 **Work in pairs.** Take turns. Use a coin to move (heads = 1 space; tails = 2 spaces). Compare and contrast as instructed.

4 **Work in groups.** Compare and contrast your parents. Are you like or unlike your parents? Do your classmates' parents seem like or unlike your own parents?

Go to page 153.

Question tags: Confirming information or seeking agreement

Alicia **is** friendly, **isn't she**?	Yes. She's outgoing. You'll like her.
You**'re** nervous about the competition, **aren't you**?	I am. I'm not sure I'm ready.
Rick **doesn't** live near here, **does he**?	No, he doesn't. He lives quite far away.
Lin also **plays** the flute, **doesn't she**?	Yes, she does. She's really good!
Sue **couldn't** make herself do it, **could she**?	No. She's too shy.

1 **Listen.** Match the questions to logical answers. Write the letter. 🎧 009

1. _____   a. Yes, it was. And we finally won!

2. _____   b. Yes, I have to be. I'm a teacher.

3. _____   c. No, she didn't. She said she was ill.

4. _____   d. He really is. He never stops!

5. _____   e. Yes, she can. And the guitar, too.

2 **Read.** Then complete the question tags.

1. Carla and Lea want to join the team, ____*don't they*____ ?

2. You're not as enthusiastic about poetry as your sister, _____ ?

3. Greg's brothers won't be at the party, _____ ?

4. Maria has changed a lot, _____ ? She's so self-confident.

5. Your sisters didn't go shopping, _____ ?

6. You would help us if Ana can't come, _____ ?

National Geographic Fellow Chef Barton Seaver

3 **Work in pairs.** Take turns forming question tags and answering them. Agree or disagree with your partner. Express your opinion.

> Barton Seaver is the most interesting chef around, isn't he?

> Yes, he really is. He has great ideas about food.

1. (name of a place) / most beautiful / place / ever
2. (name of a singer) / most popular / singer / right now
3. (name of an actor) / talented / actor / on TV
4. (name of a video game) / your favourite / video game
5. (name of a film) / exciting / film / ever

4 LEARN NEW WORDS Read about young chefs and listen to their conversation. Then listen and repeat. 🎧 010 011

Everyone loves cookery programmes! The chefs are usually self-confident and energetic, but they're not always patient or organised, are they? (That's part of the fun!) They're almost always very **competitive** as they cook against each other. They want to win by making the best food they can!

On some programmes, teen chefs compete to see who's the best cook. These teen chefs can be surprisingly **co-operative**, even while they're competing. They've made friends, and they're interested in what one another is doing. Of course, one chef may be **jealous** of another chef, but in the end many of them are still **helpful** and kind to each other as they compete. They're **open-minded** enough to know that only one person can win, but all of them can be friends – and great chefs.

5 Read. Then use a question tag to comment.

1. Angela really is a talented cook. I want to be like her!
   You aren't feeling jealous, are you?

2. Pat and Tim refused to talk to Julia, or even listen to her ideas.
   _____

3. The Whitley twins have 17 tennis trophies between them.
   _____

4. Sam won't join the group to help collect and recycle plastic bottles.
   _____

5. Here, let me help you clean up those dishes.
   _____

1 BEFORE YOU READ Discuss in pairs. Based on the title and the photo, what do you think the reading is about?

2 LEARN NEW WORDS Find the words below in the reading. What do you think they mean? Look for clues in the sentences. Then listen and repeat. ∩ 012

| bossy | ignore | perfectionist | selfish | spoilt |

3 WHILE YOU READ Notice descriptive words you think apply to you personally. ∩ 013

Why Am I Me?

Have you ever wondered why you are the way you are? What makes you different from, say, your brothers and sisters?

People have asked these questions for centuries, and researchers are trying to answer them. One idea they're exploring is that birth order influences the person we become. In general, the oldest child is described as confident, organised, dutiful and determined to get what he or she wants. Oldest children are seen as born leaders, people-pleasers and perfectionists. Because they're the oldest, their younger brothers and sisters sometimes see them as bossy, or too willing to tell other people what to do.

The middle child may be described as being competitive in order to get more attention. They sometimes feel that their family ignores them because they are in the middle. Because middle children tend to avoid conflict, they can be flexible and easygoing. They may also be seen as secretive by members of their family. They are usually more influenced by their friends than by their family, perhaps because they get more attention from their friends.

The youngest child is described as the baby of the family. They can be spoilt by their parents, who spend a lot of time with them and often give them what they want. For this reason, their brothers and sisters sometimes get jealous. Youngest children enjoy being the centre of attention, and they are seen as outgoing, open-minded and likely to take risks.

What if you're an only child? Many people think that a child with no brothers or sisters grows up wanting lots of attention. Some think they're selfish, or unwilling to share with others. But because they spend so much time around adults, they're also described as confident, determined and responsible.

4 AFTER YOU READ **Discuss the questions in groups.**

1. What's the main idea of the reading?

2. Does birth order seem like a good way to describe personality? Why or why not?

3. Based on your personal experience, does the information in this reading seem correct? If not, why not?

5 **Work in pairs.** Separately, go back through the reading and underline all the words you think describe you. Then read your list to your partner. Based on your list, can your partner guess your birth order? What is it?

6 **Work in groups.** What other factors might affect your personality? Write two or three ideas. Briefly explain how each factor on your list might affect you. Then discuss your ideas in groups.

VIDEO ▶

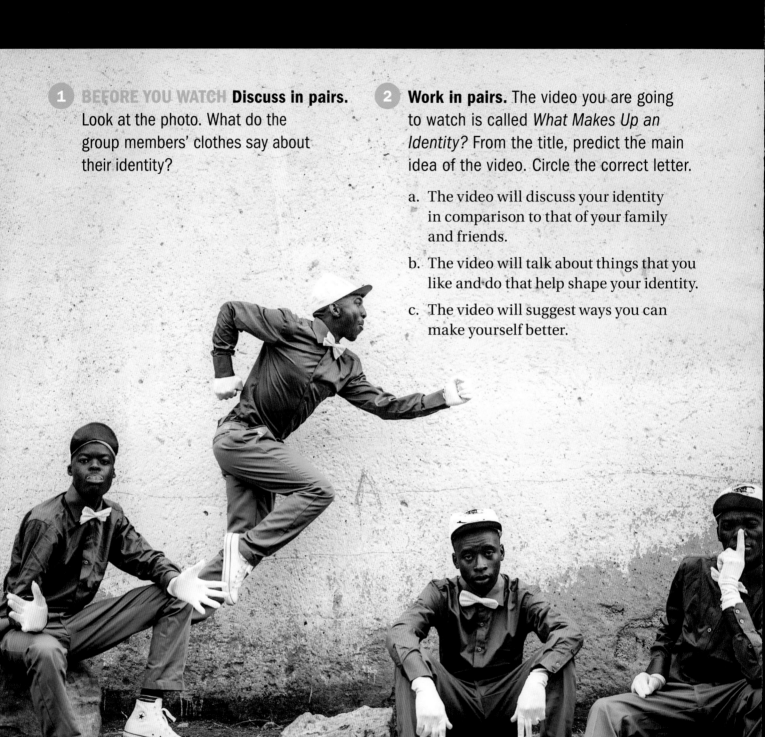

1 BEFORE YOU WATCH **Discuss in pairs.**
Look at the photo. What do the group members' clothes say about their identity?

2 **Work in pairs.** The video you are going to watch is called *What Makes Up an Identity?* From the title, predict the main idea of the video. Circle the correct letter.

a. The video will discuss your identity in comparison to that of your family and friends.

b. The video will talk about things that you like and do that help shape your identity.

c. The video will suggest ways you can make yourself better.

Rea Iktetsa Pantsula, a dance group from
Soweto, Johannesburg, South Africa

WHILE YOU WATCH **Tick the factors that the video says are important parts of your identity. Watch scene 1.1.**

☐ sports ☐ clothes ☐ gadgets ☐ food

☐ music ☐ house ☐ pets ☐ other people

4 **AFTER YOU WATCH** **Work in pairs.** Circle the correct letter.

1. According to the research, music can make us happier and _____ .
   - a. cleverer
   - b. more organised
   - c. more determined

2. A personal style is important to help you _____ .
   - a. fit in
   - b. stand out
   - c. both a and b

3. One in _____ teens is obsessed with wearing designer clothing.
   - a. two
   - b. four
   - c. twenty

4. Nearly all teenagers associate _____ with happy memories.
   - a. music
   - b. clothes
   - c. food

5. Parents help _____ .
   - a. influence our world view
   - b. choose our friends
   - c. choose our music

5 **Work in pairs.** The video describes four main areas that make up your identity. Discuss each of those areas in your own life.

6 **Discuss in groups.** At the end of the video, you're asked, 'What else makes you *you*?' Answer the question in your group. Then share your responses with the class.

7 **YOU DECIDE** **Choose an activity.**

1. **Work independently.** Choose a classmate or teacher to interview about what makes up his or her identity. Write a profile of this person and share it with the class.

2. **Work in pairs.** Write a description of your clothing in relation to your identity. Your partner does the same. Then compare your results. Does your partner have the same view of your style as you do? Discuss. Then swap roles.

3. **Work in groups.** Create a 'happy memory' cookbook. Survey at least five classmates about meals that give them happy memories. Ask the classmates to describe the meals. Take notes, and then compile the information into a cookbook to share with the class.

Using *it* to talk about weather, time and distance, and for emphasis

It's raining again. Another bad hair day! **It**'s strange that we've had so much rain.

It's six o'clock already. Wake up! I hate **it** when the alarm goes off.

It's a half-mile walk from here. We're late! **It** drives me crazy when I have to hurry.

---

1 **Listen.** How is *it* used? Write the number. 🎧 015

_____ to introduce weather _____ to introduce time

_____ to introduce distance _____ to introduce emphasis

---

2 **Work in pairs.** Write down three things that you don't like to happen. Use *it* in your sentences. Then share them with your partner.

   1. *It makes me a little angry when people interrupt me in a conversation.*

   2. _____

   3. _____

   4. _____

---

3 **Work in pairs.** Write down three things that you like to happen. Use *it* in your sentences. Then share them with your partner.

   1. *I like it when people give me compliments about my appearance.*

   2. _____

   3. _____

   4. _____

---

4 **Work in groups.** Make the cube. Take turns throwing the cube and completing the sentences.

> It drives me crazy when my friends don't return my texts!

Go to page 155.

WRITING

When we compare and contrast two people or things, we use phrases such as the following:

Compare:	**alike**	**both**	**in the same way**	**too**
Contrast:	**although**	**but**	**on the other hand**	**unlike**

1 **Read the model.** Work in pairs to identify the parts of the writing. How does the writer compare and contrast? Underline the words or phrases.

I come from a large family, and I share personality traits with several family members. But it's clear to me that I'm most like my grandfather, although we're different in some ways, too.

My grandfather and I both like spending time outside. We both enjoy riding our bikes and watching sports. We're adventurous, too. I really like going fishing with my grandfather. We'll catch our dinner together, then cook and eat it at our campsite. We both love nature. We're alike in that way. We also enjoy working in his garden growing fruit and vegetables.

It's a different story when winter comes. Unlike my grandfather, I love being outside in the snow. I like having snowball fights with my friends, but he likes sitting by the fire and reading. Sometimes he and I play cards, although I don't really enjoy that very much. I'm too energetic to sit for so long! On the other hand, when we play one of my video games, I have fun because I'm competitive. My grandfather isn't competitive at all. He's also sort of slow!

But it doesn't really matter to me what we do together. I like being with my grandfather and spending time with him. We're a good fit!

2 **Work in pairs.** How are the writer and his grandfather alike? How are they different? Do you think they're more alike than different? Explain.

3 **Write.** Compare and contrast your personality with that of a family member.

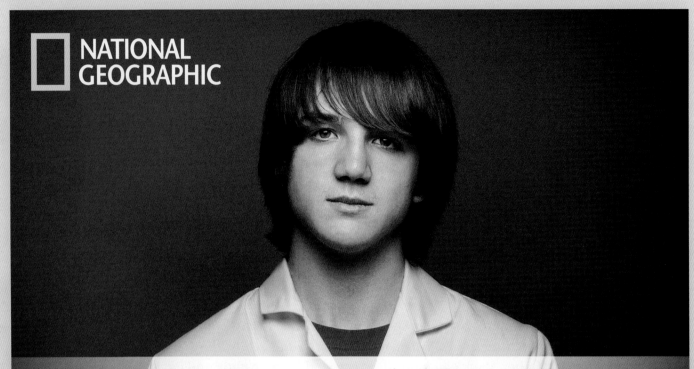

NATIONAL GEOGRAPHIC

Be Determined

'Why not you? Why can't you come up with the next great innovation or cure?'
Jack Andraka
National Geographic Explorer, Inventor

1. **Watch scene 1.2.**

2. It took Jack Andraka 4,000 tries to find a protein he needed for his experiment. It took him 200 tries to find a lab research scientist who would accept his project. What three words best describe Jack?

3. How hard do you try to get something you want or need? Do you give up easily? Would you try 200 times? 4,000 times? How would you feel if you were unsuccessful so many times?

Make an Impact

YOU DECIDE Choose a project.

① **Plan and conduct a survey about personality traits.**

- Decide which traits you want to ask about. Include positive and negative traits.
- Write the survey.
- Interview ten people. Record and report the results.

② **Plan and write a report on other factors that influence personality.**

- Search the Internet for information on your topic.
- Write your report.
- Present your research to the class.

③ **Write an advice column.**

- Write a letter to an advice columnist about a problem that young people face.
- In groups of three, read your letters aloud. Then discuss the problem and give advice. Take notes.
- Compile your group's questions and responses in an advice column. Make copies of your column to share with the class.

Misunderstood Animals

'Endangered snakes, frogs and crocodiles are not everyone's favourite. They have a special need for attention.'

Jenny Daltry

A Nile crocodile carrying its young

TO START

1. How would you describe the animals in the photo?

2. What would you do if you saw a crocodile in the wild?

3. Of the three animals Jenny Daltry mentions, which do you like the least? Why?

1 **Why do we care about some animals but not others?** Discuss. Then listen and read.

∩ 016

Why are some animals popular while others are so unpopular? In the natural world, every animal has its place and purpose. Nature doesn't judge these animals – people do. For example, it's a common misconception that snakes are **slimy** and **disgusting** to touch. Not true! A snake's skin is smooth and dry. Another misconception is that snakes are **aggressive** and will attack humans for no reason. Also untrue! Almost all snakes, even **poisonous** ones, prefer to escape or hide unless they're surprised or attacked first. Snakes are very misunderstood animals.

Snakes aren't the only animals that are misunderstood. People think that cockroaches are dirty **pests** that like to hide in dark, **filthy** places. They hate the idea that cockroaches eat rubbish and dead animals as they **decay**. People also believe cockroaches are covered in **germs**.

In fact, cockroaches clean themselves constantly, as much as cats do. They prefer to live in clean places. It's humans who, by trying to trap or **poison** cockroaches, force them to hide wherever they can in order to survive. Luckily for them, cockroaches are very hard to **destroy**. They were here on the planet before humans appeared, and they'll probably be here after we've gone!

A Borneo keeled pit viper

Cockroaches

A wasp

Wasps also have a bad reputation. Many people hate wasps because they believe that wasps **sting** humans at a moment's notice. Actually, most wasp species don't sting at all. Those that do sting are generally protecting their young, or responding to humans who shout or swing their hands at the wasp. Some wasp species do sting caterpillars, spiders and other insects. When stinging, the wasps inject their eggs into their living prey. The wasp larvae live inside and, when they're ready to leave, they eat their way out!

Should we care about these misunderstood species? Yes, we should! Every animal species plays a **crucial** role in the **ecosystem**. Some help **control** other pest populations. Some help pollinate flowers. Some eat mildew and mould, and others protect food crops. Some help contribute to medical research. Even misunderstood animals are necessary, and in many ways they're **beneficial** to humans.

2 LEARN NEW WORDS **Listen and repeat.**
   ∩ 017

3 **Work in pairs.** Did you like animals as a young child? Which animals were you afraid of? Describe them. Why were you afraid of them?

4 **Read and write the words from the list.**

beneficial	crucial	destroy	disgusting
ecosystem	poisonous	slimy	sting

A Siamese crocodile

At the age of eight, Jenny Daltry knew that she wanted to be a conservation biologist. She grew up collecting unusual animals, such as lizards, frogs and snakes. Some people think such animals are _____ or _____ . But they play a _____ role in the _____ . For example, Siamese crocodiles live in Cambodia, where they dig out the marshes to hold water during the dry season. Some people want to _____ the crocodiles, but the water would dry up and other animals would have no water to drink. So, as Jenny Daltry reminds us, even scary crocodiles are _____ .

5 **LEARN NEW WORDS Listen to these words and match them to the definitions. Then listen and repeat.** 🎧 018 019

misconception	misunderstood	unpopular	untrue

_____ 1. not a fact

_____ 2. seen by others as different from how someone or something really is

_____ 3. not liked by a large number of people

_____ 4. a wrong idea that people believe

6 **YOU DECIDE Choose an activity.**

1. **Work independently.** Choose one of the animals in the list below. Design a new look for the animal so that it doesn't seem so disgusting or unpleasant. What can you change? Think about the animal's size, colour and other physical details.

2. **Work in pairs.** Together, choose one of these animals: mosquitoes, rats, spiders or worms. Separately, describe the animal in a word web. Then compare your word web with your partner's.

3. **Work in groups.** Rank the animals below from most misunderstood (1) to least misunderstood (5). Explain your group's ranking.

cockroaches	rats	snakes	spiders	wasps

A blue-ringed octopus

SPEAKING STRATEGY 🎧020

Expressing surprise	Expressing disbelief
Wow! Really?	Oh, come on! You can't be serious.
That's <u>amazing</u>!	That's hard to believe.
No way! You're joking!	Are you sure about that?

1 **Listen.** How do the speakers express surprise and disbelief? Write the phrases you hear. 🎧021

2 **Read and complete the dialogue.**

John: This video game is full of fun facts about animals.

Mimi: Oh, really? Like what?

John: Like the fact that spiders have got six or eight eyes.

Mimi: _____

John: Yeah, I'm sure. I looked it up. Here's another one. Honeybees die after their first sting.

Mimi: _____ Well, I know a fact about bees. They communicate through different dances.

John: _____ Look at this one about bees. They've got hair on their eyes!

Mimi: _____ I know one about eyes. Did you know the colossal squid has got eyes 30 cm. (11 in.) wide?

John: _____

3 **Work in groups.** Cut out the cards. Take turns reading them aloud. Group members should express surprise or disbelief.

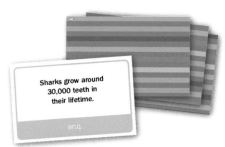

Sharks grow around 30,000 teeth in their lifetime.

true

4 **Work in pairs.** Take turns telling a surprising story about yourself that may be true or untrue. Your partner will express surprise or disbelief and then decide if your story is true or false.

Go to page 157.

Modals: Speculating about the past

could have (not sure)	They cancelled their hiking plans. They **could have read** about that escaped bear.
might have (not sure)	He refuses to go in the water. He **might have seen** a jellyfish.
may have (fairly sure)	She won't get out of the car now. She **may have heard** the neighbour's dogs fighting.
must have (very sure)	They took her to hospital immediately. That spider **must have been** poisonous.

1 **Listen.** How sure are the speakers about their ideas? Write *not sure, fairly sure* or *very sure*. 🎧 **023**

1. _____ 2. _____ 3. _____

4. _____ 5. _____ 6. _____

2 **Read and write.** For each item, write a sentence speculating about the past. Use *could have, may have, might have* and *must have* in your sentences.

1. Alice went into the kitchen for a midnight snack. She turned on the light and screamed. _____

2. Don kept scratching his arms and legs all night. _____

_____

3. Julia heard something running inside the walls. _____

_____

4. Ken found the litter bin on its side. There was rubbish all over the pavement.

_____

3 **Work in pairs.** Take turns speculating about the past. Use *could have, may have, might have* and *must have* in your sentences.

1. She cried all night.
2. They ran as fast as they could.
3. He got really angry.
4. She screamed after biting into her sandwich.

Caribbean giant cockroaches

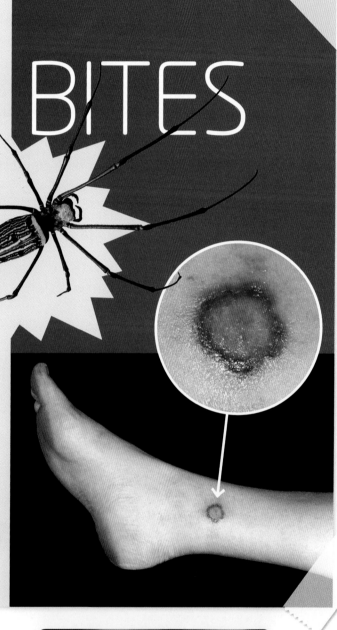

BE PREPARED.
SPIDER BITES

Are you **scared of** spider bites? Learn what to do.

- Do you have a spider **bite**?
- Spider bites can **hurt** a lot.
- Stay **calm**. Try not to get **upset**.
- If you think the bite is from a poisonous spider, don't move. Moving makes the **venom** go through your body faster.
- Wash the bite with soap and water. Then apply a cloth with cold water or ice to the bite.
- If the bite is on a hand, arm or leg, keep the bite area above the level of your heart.

CALL FOR HELP IMMEDIATELY.

Emperor scorpion

5 **Work in pairs.** Look at the poster again. The same advice is good for some scorpions, too. Take turns describing what to do if you're stung by a scorpion.

6 **Work in groups.** Imagine that your friend showed you a bite on his arm. Speculate about what happened. Use *could have, may have, might have* and *must have* in your sentences.

BEFORE YOU READ Discuss in pairs. What do you know about bats? Make a two-column table. Write five things you think are true in the left-hand column.

2 **LEARN NEW WORDS Find these words in the reading.** What do you think they mean? Use a thesaurus to check. Then listen and repeat. ⌒ 026

fangs	lethal	lick	myth	suck

3 WHILE YOU READ **Notice details that support the beliefs you listed in Activity 1.** ⌒ 027

4 AFTER YOU READ **Work in pairs to answer the questions.**

1. What is the main idea of the article?
2. How many species of bats are there?
3. What are some myths about bats?
4. Where do vampire bats get the blood they need?
5. How are vampire bats beneficial?

5 **Find details to support your beliefs.** Look at your table from Activity 1. Next to each of your beliefs about bats, write any details from the reading that support those beliefs.

Vampire Bats

ARE HUMANS RIGHT TO FEAR ALL THINGS VAMPIRE?

There are around 1,200 species of bats on the planet. Most of them eat insects or fruit. Some bats eat scorpions, frogs or other small animals. But there are some bats that aren't interested in any of those foods. These are the often-feared vampire bats. And yes, it's true! Vampire bats do need to drink blood to survive!

Why are so many people scared of bats? They're scared in part because there are so many myths, or false stories, about bats. One myth is that bats are flying mice. Another is that bats are blind, and so they can get caught in your hair. But the most popular myth, by far, is the one that connects vampire bats and the scary, fictional creatures known as vampires.

In novels, films and television programmes, fictional vampires use their sharp fangs to bite people in the neck and then suck their blood. Real vampire bats do have fangs. They use them to make small cuts in an animal's skin, but they don't suck blood through their fangs. Instead, they wait until blood starts flowing from the cut. Then they lick the blood with their tongues, just as a kitten drinks milk from a bowl.

Vampire bats get blood from birds, cows, horses and other farm animals. They can drink gently from a sleeping animal for half an hour without waking it. Their bite isn't lethal, and the blood loss doesn't hurt the animals.

Vampire bats can live for about two days without drinking blood. This is usually plenty of time to look for food. And, unless there's no other food source available, a vampire bat won't bite a human. In general, vampire bats are comfortable, and sometimes even friendly, around humans.

In addition, vampire bats are a valuable source of information for medical research. While they're drinking blood, these bats release substances that help blood keep flowing as they drink. Scientists are studying vampire bats to see if they can develop medications that work in the same way. Their research could one day help people with circulation problems or medical conditions such as heart attacks and strokes.

6 Discuss in groups.

1. Even after they've learnt that bats are beneficial, some people still don't like them. Why do you think that is?

2. Why do you think people like the idea of vampires so much? Do you have a favourite vampire character? Who is it? Why is this particular vampire your favourite?

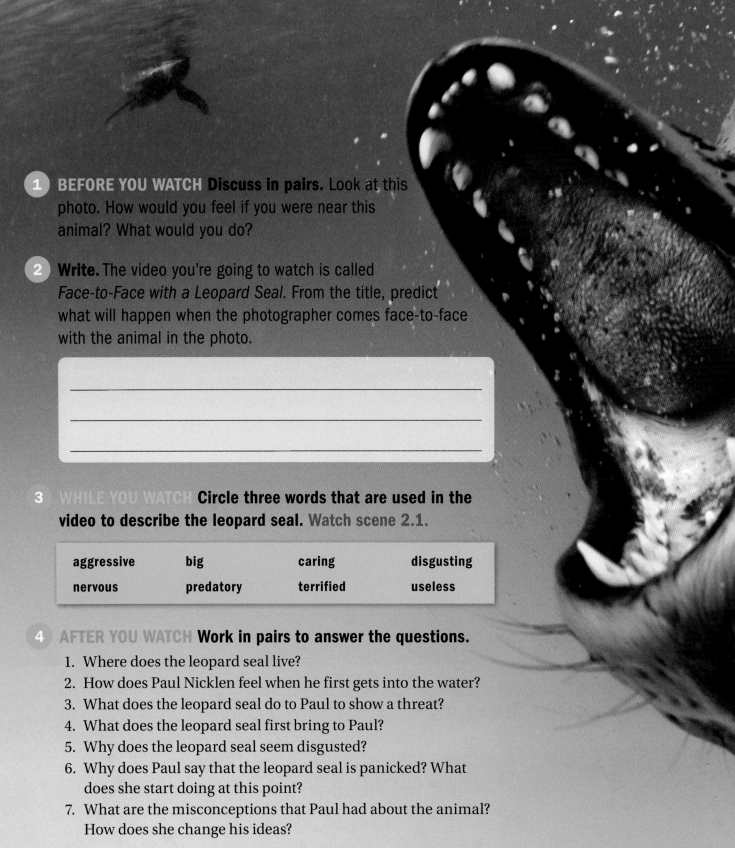

1 **BEFORE YOU WATCH Discuss in pairs.** Look at this photo. How would you feel if you were near this animal? What would you do?

2 **Write.** The video you're going to watch is called *Face-to-Face with a Leopard Seal.* From the title, predict what will happen when the photographer comes face-to-face with the animal in the photo.

_____

_____

_____

3 **WHILE YOU WATCH Circle three words that are used in the video to describe the leopard seal.** Watch scene 2.1.

aggressive	big	caring	disgusting
nervous	predatory	terrified	useless

4 **AFTER YOU WATCH Work in pairs to answer the questions.**

1. Where does the leopard seal live?
2. How does Paul Nicklen feel when he first gets into the water?
3. What does the leopard seal do to Paul to show a threat?
4. What does the leopard seal first bring to Paul?
5. Why does the leopard seal seem disgusted?
6. Why does Paul say that the leopard seal is panicked? What does she start doing at this point?
7. What are the misconceptions that Paul had about the animal? How does she change his ideas?

A leopard seal

5 **Work in pairs.** Look at your answers from Activity 2. Did you correctly predict the outcome of the video? Explain how the leopard seal's actions help classify it as a misunderstood animal.

6 **Discuss in groups.** Why do you think Paul wanted to photograph the leopard seal? What can he teach others about this animal with his photos and his story? Explain, using examples from the video.

7 **YOU DECIDE** **Choose an activity.**

1. **Work independently.** Research leopard seals. Learn about their role in the Antarctic ecosystem. What animals do they prey on? Who are their predators? Prepare a short presentation to share with the class.

2. **Work in pairs.** Compare and contrast the leopard seal with another misunderstood animal from this unit. Use a Venn diagram to show the two animals' similarities and differences.

3. **Work in groups.** Many people consider the leopard seal a dangerous, deadly predator. Create an advertisement to educate people about the leopard seal and persuade them to change their opinions.

Infinitives with and without *to*

To hold a rat is scary!   I can't **hold** one!

He doesn't want **to hold** rats.   Make him **try** it.

She's excited **to hold** one.   We'll watch her **do** it.

That's the rat **to get**!   OK. I'll let her **buy** it.

She's going to the pet shop **to buy** it.   I'll even help her **pay** for it.

1   **Read.** Circle the correct letter.

1. My brother really wants _____ get a pet rat.

    a. ⊘   b. to

2. My mother will absolutely not let him _____ buy one.

    a. ⊘   b. to

3. He's planning _____ save money for one anyway.

    a. ⊘   b. to

4. I can't wait _____ see what happens when Mum finds out.

    a. ⊘   b. to

5. She'll make him _____ take it back to the shop.

    a. ⊘   b. to

6. I really want _____ see him get in trouble instead of me!

    a. ⊘   b. to

A rat

2   **Work in pairs.** Play Noughts and Crosses. Use infinitives with or without *to* in your sentences. One of you is X; the other is O.

I might touch a hairy spider!

Not me! I can't do it!

might	can't	have
make	want	help
watch	feel	ask

Ants

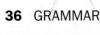

A process description explains how something is done or how something happens. The purpose of the steps and the order in which they happen are described.

Purpose:	in order to	so that		
Sequence:	before	during	after	finally
	first	then	next	while
	little by little	meanwhile	over time	

1 **Read the model.** Work in pairs to identify the process being described. What words and phrases does the writer use to show purpose and sequence? Underline them.

When you're very, very afraid of something, that fear can affect you and how you live your life. When I was younger, I saw my cousin fall onto an ants' nest. The ants attacked him, and he was covered in horrible bites. After that, I became very scared of ants. I wouldn't eat outside, and I didn't even like playing outside. I checked my bed for ants every night. But when I turned 13, I decided I couldn't let my fear get to me. I had to learn to control my fear of ants.

First, I read a lot about different ants. I didn't focus on bites, but instead I read about how beneficial ants are to the planet. Ants are really cool! They're hard-working, social and organised. They help bring air and nutrients to the soil. They pollinate plants, clean up decaying matter and help control other insects.

Next, I began to watch ants from a safe distance. I started to look at a colony of ants in real time on the Internet in order to learn how they live. Little by little, I felt more comfortable about ants. Finally, I went outside one day and let an ant crawl onto my hand. It was OK! Now that I know about all the good things ants do, I'm not so afraid of them any more.

LIVE   Live feed of an ant farm

2 **Work in pairs.** Imagine you're scared of an insect or animal. What steps would you take if you wanted to control your fear? Why?

3 **Write.** Many people are scared of pit bulls. Imagine you have a new pit bull puppy. You don't want it to be misunderstood. How will you train it to be a good dog? Describe the process. How could you help people to understand your dog better?

Keep an Open Mind

'To me, it's symbolic. If you don't care about this particular snake, why should you care about anything else? Each one is part of a great web.'

Jenny Daltry
National Geographic Explorer, Herpetologist and Conservationist

1. **Watch scene 2.2.**

2. What can you do to learn more about misunderstood animals?

3. How can you help other people understand misunderstood animals?

Make an Impact

YOU DECIDE Choose a project.

1 **Make a set of misunderstood-animal cards.**

· Choose at least five misunderstood animals to research. Find two or three facts that might help clear up misunderstandings about the animals.

· Write information about the animal on one side of the card. Include a photo or drawing and caption on the other side.

· Present your cards to the class.

2 **Plan and produce an animal quiz show for TV.**

· Decide on the format of your quiz show.

· Research and prepare questions about animals for competing teams.

· Act out and film the show.

3 **Educate others about misunderstood animals.**

· Collect information about a group of misunderstood animals.

· Make informational posters or fact sheets.

· Display the posters in your school or hand out the fact sheets to students and teachers.

A jumping spider

Express Yourself

1   **Read and listen to the story.** ∩ 029

A Day in the Life

Well, finally something is happening, Kim thought. So far, it had been the most boring summer ever. School was starting in less than a week, and she had nothing interesting to report to her classmates. Suddenly, loud beeps, warning that a lorry is backing up, broke the afternoon silence. Kim held her bottle of cold water against her forehead as she walked over to the bushes that separated her house from the one next door.

I hope the new neighbours are cool, she thought as she looked at the stacks of boxes outside the lorry. *Let's see. Lots of boxes! That one says, 'kitchen stuff' and that one says, 'Jane's stuff'. Wow, what a huge TV! Oh, a keyboard. I wonder who plays that. That box says, 'Jane's trophies'. Hmm. I wonder who Jane is. And look at that, a water bowl with the name Cupcake on it.*

Maybe they have a cat, thought Kim. And then she saw a long pink lead tied to one of the handles on the back door of the lorry. Whatever was on the other end of the lead was under the lorry, staying out of the hot sun. And it probably wasn't a cat!

Kim stepped around the bushes to get a better look. 'Here, Cupcake. Come here, girl!' she called. She poured some of her water into the bowl and called again. 'Here, Cupcake. Come on out, little girl.'

Kim heard something move. A large dog crawled out from under the lorry and then stood up and shook itself. 'Well, look at you,' Kim said. 'You're not a little girl, are you? But you look so sweet! Are you thirsty? Here, have some water.'

It was after the dog had finished the water and was happily licking Kim's hand that she looked up.

'I see you've met Cupcake,' said a girl she'd never met before. 'I'm Jane.'

'I'm Kim,' she said. 'Nice to meet you. Welcome to the neighbourhood.'

They'd barely started talking when Kim heard someone shouting. From the other side of the bushes, her mum shouted, 'That dog's a *pit bull*, Kim. Get over here right now before that dog *bites* you! Those dogs are so *aggressive*. Come *here*!'

'Mum,' Kim said calmly. '*Relax*. She's so friendly and sweet. Her name's Cupcake!'

'I don't *care* what its name is. Come home *now!*'

Kim looked at Jane, and then looked down at her feet, not sure of what to say next.

'Go ahead,' Jane said. 'We can talk later. And maybe you can show me how to get to school.'

'Sure, Jane. I'd like that. And maybe we can take Cupcake for a walk.'

Well, Kim thought as she returned home. *Maybe the rest of the summer won't be so boring after all.*

2 **Work in groups.** Discuss the questions.

1. What happens in the story?

2. What are some of the misconceptions in the story?

3. Kim's mum probably embarrassed her in front of Jane. Why are teens sometimes embarrassed by their parents? Do the parents know they're doing it? Explain.

3 **Connect ideas.** In Unit 1, you learnt how people can misunderstand others and be misunderstood. In Unit 2, you learnt about misunderstood animals. In both situations, people are involved. What does this tell you about the way we think? About our misconceptions?

4 **YOU DECIDE** Choose an activity.

1. Choose a topic:
   • no one understands me
   • no one understands (animal)

2. Choose a way to express yourself:
   • a short story
   • a song or a poem
   • a video

3. Present your work.

Everybody's Doing It!

'There is socially contagious behaviour when you're in a crowd.'

Iain Couzin

A group of nearly 2,000 kayaks and canoes

TO START

1. Look at the photo. What are the people doing? Do you think they meant to do this? Explain.

2. Think about a time when you were in a large group like the one in the photo. What was going on? Why were you and all the other people there?

3. According to Iain Couzin, when we're in a group, we tend to act like the others in the group. Do you agree with him? Why or why not? Give examples.

1 **Humans usually make their own choices about joining groups. Do you think animals can make these same choices?** Discuss. Then listen and read. ∩ **030**

We've all looked up at the sky to see a group of birds flying together. We might see noisy geese flying in a V-shaped **formation** as they **migrate** to a warmer climate, or a spiral of starlings at sunset. Or, unfortunately, we may have seen a group of mosquitoes or wasps coming at us! On land, we might see a group of wild horses running free, or a group of dogs in a field, or a group of monkeys in trees. Underwater, we might see a group of fish swimming together in sudden but perfectly **co-ordinated** movement.

A group of fish swimming
away from a sailfish

Most groups that humans **belong to** have **leaders**. Sometimes, though, we may be in crowds with no leaders, as in a stadium full of sports fans. Can we **assume** that animal groups act in the same way? In the case of elephants, the oldest female is the leader. All her offspring, or young, and their offspring remain with her for many years. But in the case of fish that assemble in groups, there is no one leader. The fish come to an agreement together through **consensus**. They see what their neighbours are doing and mimic their behaviour. If they see a **potential** predator, they will all quickly swim away together to avoid it. Any fish that **prefer** to go off alone are probably going to be lunch!

Scientists now **realise** that **collective** behaviour in animals is a highly **efficient system** that is beneficial in many ways. These group behaviours allow animals to complete their **migrations** in relative safety, find food and protect group members from predators.

2 LEARN NEW WORDS **Listen and repeat.** ∩ 031

3 **Work in pairs.** Can you think of other animals that belong to groups with leaders? Other animals that belong to groups without leaders? Make a list for each type of animal. Share your lists with the class.

4 Read and circle the correct word.

Iain Couzin liked animals as a child, but it was as an adult that he decided to focus on *efficient / collective* behaviours in animals. He came to *realise / assume* that, unlike the rhino or leopard, not all animals *prefer / migrate* to live or hunt alone. He discovered that many animals have highly *potential / coordinated*, complex social *systems / consensus* that permit them to do things as a group that they could never do alone. His studies on birds, fish and insects allow scientists to find *potential / assumed* solutions to problems such as how humans affect animal habitats, oil spills and even world hunger.

5 LEARN NEW WORDS Listen to these words and match them to their synonyms. Then listen and repeat. ∩ 032 033

assemble	crowd	mimic	remain

_____ 1. group

_____ 2. stay

_____ 3. imitate

_____ 4. come together

6 YOU DECIDE Choose an activity. Work in pairs.

1. Why do animals remain in groups? What are the advantages? Are there any disadvantages? Make two lists.

2. Some animal behaviours seem unselfish. Individual members will put the good of the group above their own. Describe an example.

3. You want to form a group at school. What are three rules that group members would have to follow? Why are those rules important?

Expressing cause	Expressing effect
Since she's scared of wasps, we stayed inside.	She's scared of wasps, so we stayed inside.
Because of the lack of food, the animals had to travel further and further away.	There was a lack of food. As a result, the animals had to travel further and further away.
The experiment was called off due to the poor weather conditions.	The weather conditions were poor. Consequently, the experiment was called off.

1 **Listen.** How do the speakers express cause and effect? Write the words and phrases you hear. 🎧035

2 **Read and complete the dialogue.**

Alex: Iain and his team worked with army ants, too.

Billy: What did they want to find out?

Alex: _____ ants are so social, the team wanted to see how they organise their collective behaviours.

Billy: Don't they live together in huge groups?

Alex: Yeah, and _____ , they have to be really organised.

Billy: It makes sense, I guess, _____ their numbers.

Alex: Yes, there are usually tens of thousands of ants moving at one time. _____ potential traffic jams, they organise a kind of super-motorway.

Billy: And, _____ , everyone keeps moving?

Alex: Yes! The ants with food use a wide middle lane, and the ants that aren't carrying anything form lanes on the side.

3 **Work in groups.** Take turns. Use a coin to move (heads = 1 space; tails = 2 spaces). Express cause or effect.

4 **Work in pairs.** Humans are harming many habitats. What are some reasons for this?

Go to page 159.

GRAMMAR 🎧 036

Two-word verbs

Separable

The scientists **talked over** the problem.
The scientists **talked** the problem **over**.
The scientists **talked** it **over**.

They **worked out** a solution.
They **worked** a solution **out**.
They **worked** it **out**.

Inseparable

The scientists **talked about** the problem.
The scientists **talked about** it.

The scientists **looked into** the evidence.
The scientists **looked into** it.

1 **Read and complete the sentences.** Make any necessary changes.

apply to	calm down	cheer up	count on
hold back	look at	turn out	work out

Humans love to laugh. In fact, even hearing other people laugh can _____*cheer*_____ us _____*up*_____ or make us smile. But sometimes, even when it isn't appropriate, we just can't help ourselves and we start laughing, too! Who hasn't seen people trying hard to stop giggling and to _____ themselves _____ in a place where they should be quiet?

Yawning is another common contagious behaviour. When you _____ someone who's yawning, you usually want to yawn, too. Can you _____ that yawn _____ ? Probably not. It's very hard to resist the urge!

Did you know that even animals yawn? It _____ that chimpanzees, dogs, lions and other animals yawn when an animal in their group yawns.

Why are these behaviours so contagious? Scientists think they have _____ the answer _____ . They believe the same reason _____ both behaviours. They are old, basic ways to show a social connection with others in your group.

2 **Read the text in Activity 1 again.** Circle four sentences with separable verbs. Two can be rewritten without separating the verb. Write them below.

_____

_____

3 **LEARN NEW WORDS Do you think gorillas and wolves can yawn contagiously?** Listen. Then listen and repeat. 🎧 037 038

a **troop** of gorillas

a **flock** of birds

a **herd** of elephants

a **swarm** of ants

a **pack** of wolves

a **school** of fish

4 **Work in pairs.** Go back to page 44. Take turns reading sentences in the first paragraph aloud. Each time you see the word _group_, say one of the words in Activity 3 instead.

5 **Work in groups.** Listen again. Then take turns using verbs from the list to summarise the information. 🎧 039

build up	carry out	clean up	rely on	respond to

6 **Work in pairs.** Talk about three surprising things you have learnt about contagious behaviour. Use some verbs from the list.

calm down	cheer up	respond to	think about	turn out	work out

1 **BEFORE YOU READ Discuss in pairs.** The title of the reading is *Humans in Groups*. What groups do you belong to? Make a list.

2 **LEARN NEW WORDS Find these words in the reading.** What do you think they mean? Use the context to help you. Then listen and repeat. 🎧 040

| flash mob | influence | intention | join | stand out |

3 **WHILE YOU READ Notice definitions and examples in the text.** 🎧 041

4 **AFTER YOU READ Work in small groups to answer the questions.**

1. What is the main idea of the reading?

2. What are some kinds of groups mentioned in the reading?

3. Why do people want to join groups?

4. How are in-groups and out-groups different?

5. What are emergent groups? Have you ever belonged to an emergent group? Explain what happened.

5 **Define words.** Choose five words or phrases from the reading. Make a two-column table. Write the word or phrase on the left and its definition on the right.

A flash mob in Bucharest, Romania

Humans in Groups

You and all humans belong to many kinds of groups. In some, membership is involuntary – that is, you were not part of the decision to belong. For example, if you were born in Peru, you are a member of the group Peruvians. Other examples of involuntary group membership include left-handed people or brown-eyed people.

Most of the time, though, you and the rest of us want to join, or become members of, certain groups. Why? Joining the technology club, the school choir, or a volunteer group that visits people in hospital reflects your interests and becomes part of your social identity. You become an accepted member of the chosen in-group. At the same time, you remain different from the out-group, those people who are not in the group. This reflects the human desire to belong, but also the desire to stand out, or be seen as different.

Most groups we join have the intention of lasting over time. They work to influence others in some way. But sometimes emergent groups form without goals or structure. The members of emergent groups don't know each other, but come together suddenly to respond to an event. For instance, a group of people might see a car accident and immediately come together to help the victims.

Not all short-lived groups deal with accidents or disasters. A flash mob, which is a group of people who suddenly assemble to perform in public, only comes together for a short time and then disappears. The goal of a flash mob is to do something surprising and entertaining in public, such as having a pillow fight or dancing in the street.

Whether we're fighting with pillows or helping people, humans are social beings who come together in groups.

6 **Discuss in groups.**

1. Go back to your own list of the groups you named in Activity 1. What kinds of groups were named? Compare and contrast the groups.

2. In Unit 1, you learnt about your personal identity. In this unit, you learnt about your social identity as a member of groups. How do these two identities influence one another? Give an example.

3. Would you like to be in a flash mob? What would you want the flash mob to do?

VIDEO ▶

1 BEFORE YOU WATCH Discuss in pairs. Compare your own abilities with those of an ant. Name something an ant can do that you cannot.

2 Read and circle. The video you're going to watch is called *Smarter by the Swarm*. The video is about swarm intelligence. Can you guess what that means? Circle the letter.

   a. the ability of people to pressure each other into doing something

   b. improved knowledge and ability that comes when organisms work together

   c. ants living in a colony

3 WHILE YOU WATCH Note two benefits of ants working together. Watch scene 3.1.

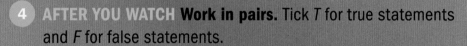

4 AFTER YOU WATCH Work in pairs. Tick *T* for true statements and *F* for false statements.

1. Your brain is about 4,000 times larger than an ant's brain.   Ⓣ Ⓕ

2. Ants often look lost when they're in large groups.   Ⓣ Ⓕ

3. Ants leave a scent that sends a message to other ants in the colony.   Ⓣ Ⓕ

4. Ants can communicate the fastest route to get to a place.   Ⓣ Ⓕ

5. Companies are mimicking ant behaviour to be more efficient.   Ⓣ Ⓕ

6. These companies learnt that ant behaviour isn't effective in humans.   Ⓣ Ⓕ

5 Work in pairs. What is *swarm intelligence*? Describe the meaning of this term. Use examples from ants and people in your answer. Then go back to Activity 2. Did you have the correct answer?

6 Discuss in groups. Think about shipping, transport and airlines. Why is it important for vehicles to work together? What do you think happens if a lorry, boat or plane doesn't communicate with others in its group? Compare this with what happens if an ant doesn't communicate with the rest of its colony.

A group of weaver ants work together to carry a drop of water back to their nest.

7 YOU DECIDE Choose an activity.

1. **Work independently.** Create a comic strip with ants as the main characters. Your comic strip should show both individual and group behaviour with ants.

2. **Work in pairs.** Find out about a team of people who work together to solve problems. Explain who's on the team and what each person's role is. Share your answers with the class.

3. **Work in groups.** Imagine that you're a team of researchers and you have a group of microbots. Develop a project idea for how they can work together to get something done. Explain the goal of the project and how the microbots would make it happen.

GRAMMAR 🎧042

***Enough, too many, too much*: Talking about amounts**

I've got **enough** pillows, but there are **not enough** feathers. I need more.

You've put **too many** in each pillow. We've run out of feathers.

Do you want to join the flash mob pillow fight?

No way. All those people and feathers, too? It's **too much** stress for me.

1 **Listen.** For each sentence you hear, tick the correct amount. 🎧043

	less than needed	the right amount	more than needed
1.	☐	☐	☐
2.	☐	☐	☐
3.	☐	☐	☐
4.	☐	☐	☐

2 **Read and complete the dialogue.**

Carlos: Do you want to join our flash mob later? Right now, we haven't got _____ people participating.

Juan: No, thanks. I've got _____ things to do this afternoon.

Carlos: You haven't got _____ time to see Gloria? She'll be there.

Juan: Really? OK then, I'll do my errands afterward. They shouldn't take _____ time.

3 **Work in groups of three.** Take turns playing *Rock, Paper, Scissors.* The winner chooses one item from list A and one from list B. Then the winner chooses another player to make a sentence with the chosen items. Each correct sentence is worth 1 point. The player with the most points at the end wins.

LIST A:	LIST B:
enough	dancers
not enough	money
too many	people
too much	time
	pillows

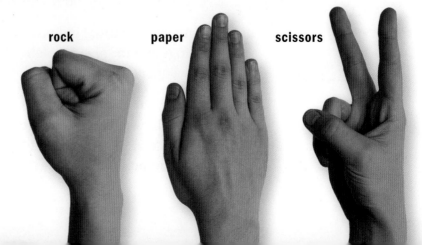

rock   paper   scissors

In writing, using good examples is one way to explain and support the main idea. We can introduce examples with phrases such as:

for example   **for instance**   **in other words**   **such as**

1. **Read the model.** Work in pairs to identify the parts of the writing. How does the writer introduce examples? Underline the phrases.

Sometimes I like being alone, but I usually prefer being with my friends. My friends and I enjoy being together because we're interested in a lot of the same things. For instance, we all like sports, and most of us play on the school football team. We also ride our bikes to places we like, such as the park.

But our favourite thing is going shopping on Saturdays. We like looking in the shops, but we have fun doing crazy things, too. In other words, we like to get people's attention. For example, we might all wear one blue sock and one red sock to see if anyone notices. Or we might pretend to look for a lost contact lens on the floor to see if someone else will start looking.

Once, we made up a foreign-sounding language and pretended that we were tourists from another country. We had a map and pretended to ask for directions in our fake language. But it was so funny, we couldn't stop laughing. Unfortunately, by now most people at the shopping centre know us, so they just ignore us!

2. **Work in pairs.** What examples of group behaviour does the writer describe? Are any of them contagious group behaviour? If so, which ones?

3. **Write.** Choose a human group behaviour or an animal group behaviour. Write a description of this behaviour. Make sure you include several examples.

Collaborate

'From invasive cells to schooling fish to human cultures, groups can accomplish what solitary individuals cannot.'

Iain Couzin
National Geographic Explorer, Behavioural Ecologist

1. **Watch scene 3.2.**

2. Iain studies group behaviour of birds, insects, fish and other animals. What other group behaviours could we learn from?

3. When is it better to work alone? To work in a group? Name something that you accomplished as a group member that you couldn't have done alone.

Make an Impact

YOU DECIDE Choose a project.

1 **Plan and carry out a flash mob activity.**

· Choose an activity to carry out as a flash mob.

· Notify people on social media about the time and place of your flash mob.

· Film your flash mob and present it to the class.

2 **Plan and make a video of human group behaviour.**

· With a group, go to a crowded place. Pretend to look for something on the floor, such as a contact lens.

· One group member should film what happens for two or three minutes. Take notes on any contagious behaviour.

· Write the results of your experiment, and present them to the class.

3 **Plan and carry out a photo shoot in nature.**

· Choose a local insect or bird to observe.

· Research its group behaviours and take photos.

· Write and present a report to the class.

'When you buy a piece of clothing, there should be a personal connection.'

Asher Jay

Fashion Footprints

Boys in São Paolo, Brazil

TO START

1. Are these boys dressed the same? Discuss the similarities and differences.

2. Do you choose the clothes you wear? Why do you wear the clothes you do?

3. Do you have a personal connection with all of the clothes you wear? Why or why not?

1 **Why do people wear the clothes they wear?**
Discuss. Then listen and read. ⌒ **044**

There are many different reasons we buy and wear the clothes we do. We choose clothes for practical reasons, such as weather and comfort. We also wear the clothes we do for psychological reasons. These include wanting to feel powerful, to feel attractive and to show our **creativity** and personality. Wearing certain **styles** affects how we feel about ourselves and how other people see us. We may care about the latest **trendy** fashion by popular **designers**, or we may prefer practical clothes.

And finally we make our clothing choices for social reasons, such as showing we want to **fit in** with a group, or making a statement about our beliefs.

The environment is another reason that clothing choice is important. The clothes we buy and wear **have an impact** on the planet. This is known as our fashion **footprint**. Each one of us has our own individual footprint. We need to **take responsibility for** our clothing decisions and **do our part** to reduce our fashion footprints.

These Japanese teens show off their accessories in Harajuku Square.

crop

cotton

Cotton uses more pesticides than any **crop** in the world.

A lot of our clothing is made from natural **materials** such as **cotton**, wool, leather and silk. **Synthetic** materials, such as nylon and polyester, are also very popular. But all of these materials, whether natural or synthetic, affect the environment. For example, many **toxic** **chemicals** are used to make leather shoes. The **manufacture** of cotton jeans requires enormous amounts of water and energy. And if dyes are used to colour any of these materials, then even more water, energy and toxic chemicals are required.

2 **LEARN NEW WORDS Listen and repeat.** 🎧 045

3 **Work in pairs.** Talk about what's in your wardrobe. Describe the materials your clothes are made of. What is your favourite outfit? How often do you wear it?

4 **Read and write the words from the list.** Make any necessary changes.

cotton	creativity	designer	fit in
manufacture	style	take responsibility for	trendy

Asher Jay has a great sense of _____ , but she also cares about our planet. She's a fashion _____ , or a person who designs clothes. She's also an artist, writer and environmental activist. Asher wants us all to _____ protecting the environment and animals. In one fashion line, she created _____ shirts, dresses and skirts influenced by the bright oranges and greens of endangered coral reefs. For Asher, fashion is more than an effort to _____ with a crowd. She believes the clothes you wear can communicate both a message you care about and your own _____ .

5 **LEARN NEW WORDS Listen to these words and match them to the definitions.** Then listen and repeat. 🎧 046 047

attractive	popular	psychological	social

_____ 1. mental

_____ 2. having a quality that people like

_____ 3. related to people being with one another

_____ 4. liked by many people

6 **YOU DECIDE Choose an activity. Work in pairs.**

1. Some schools require students to wear uniforms. What social or psychological reasons might they have for doing this?

2. Discuss. Do you dress more for yourself or for the impression you might make on others? Do you and your friends dress in a similar way? Is it better to fit in or to stand out? Why?

3. Do a video interview. Ask your classmates about their favourite outfits and why they like them.

Asher's T-shirt has illustrations of plastic rubbish in the shape of a whale's tail.

SPEAKING STRATEGY 🎧048

Asking for clarification	Clarifying
When you say _____ , what do you mean?	What I meant was _____ .
Are you saying that _____ ?	That's right./No, that's not it. I meant _____ .
Could you explain that a little more?	Of course. I was referring to _____ .

1. **Listen.** How do the speakers make sure they're communicating clearly? Write the phrases you hear. 🎧049

2. **Read and complete the dialogue.**

Pat: I like to choose my clothes depending on my mood.

Ken: When you say 'mood', _____ ?

Pat: I _____ whether I feel happy, nervous, sad ... whatever.

Ken: Oh. _____ ?

Pat: _____ my feelings. When I feel really happy, I like to wear bright colours like yellow, red and orange. When I'm sad, I wear black or grey. And when I'm nervous, I wear my favourite old blue jumper, especially on exam days.

Ken: _____ it's your lucky jumper?

Pat: Yes, I guess so. It makes me feel calmer.

3. **Work in groups.** Spin the wheel and discuss, using the words for each topic as instructed. Ask for clarification and clarify as needed.

Go to page 155.

4. **Work in pairs.** How does asking for clarification and clarifying help you communicate? How can it help other people, such as doctors or teachers, communicate?

GRAMMAR 🔊 050

Present passive: Describing actions and processes

They use a lot of pesticides to grow cotton.
They make a lot of clothing from synthetic materials.

A lot of pesticides **are used** to grow cotton.
A lot of clothing **is made** from synthetic materials.

1 **Listen.** Circle all the passive forms you hear. 🔊 051

| are bought | are made | are required | are used | is made | is used |

2 **Read.** Underline all examples of the present passive.

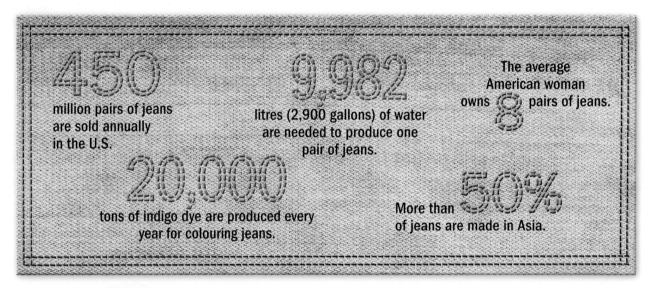

450 million pairs of jeans are sold annually in the U.S.

9,982 litres (2,900 gallons) of water are needed to produce one pair of jeans.

The average American woman owns 8 pairs of jeans.

20,000 tons of indigo dye are produced every year for colouring jeans.

More than 50% of jeans are made in Asia.

3 **Work in pairs.** Talk about how jeans are made. Change the verbs to the present passive.

1. People make jeans with a material called denim.

2. They make denim out of cotton.

3. They sometimes mix polyester or other synthetic materials into the denim.

> Jeans are made with a material called denim.

4. They dye the denim yarn before they make the denim fabric.

5. After they cut the fabric and make the jeans, they pre-wash them.

6. They sometimes add stones when they pre-wash jeans to make them look older.

4 **LEARN NEW WORDS Listen.** Learn about the journey of jeans. Then listen and repeat. 🎧 052 | 053

to ship

to assemble

factory

warehouse

retailer

to purchase

5 **Work in pairs.** Look at the infographic above.
Use the present passive to describe the journey of jeans.
Use the words in the box to describe the process.

after that	finally	first	then

6 **Work in groups.** Use the present passive to describe how something else is done or made.

1 **BEFORE YOU READ** **Discuss in pairs.** Based on the title and the photos, what do you think the reading is about?

2 **LEARN NEW WORDS Find these words in the reading.** What do you think they mean? Use a dictionary to check. Pay attention to the pronunciation of each word. Then listen and repeat. 🎧 054

donate	eco-friendly	entrepreneur
give back	profit	

3 **WHILE YOU READ Look for similarities and differences.** 🎧 055

4 **AFTER YOU READ Work in pairs to answer the questions.**

1. What's the main point of the reading?
2. What's unusual about the two designers?
3. How did Santana Draper and Maya Penn get their start?
4. What's one important reason they were successful?
5. How do the two designers use part of their profits?

5 **Compare and contrast Maya and Santana.** Use a Venn diagram to organise information.

6 **Discuss in pairs.**

1. What do you have a passion for? Music? Art? Sports? Animals? Why?

2. Santana and Maya are following their passion and finding success. Do you think it's better to follow your passion or to do something more practical?

3. Imagine you create a company and earn a lot of money. Would you use any of your profits to help people? To help the environment? Why or why not?

Santana Draper

A Passion for
FASHION

Pursuing a dream isn't just for grown-ups. These young designers grew up with a passion for fashion – and for helping others.

Santana Draper is a young entrepreneur with a giving spirit. When he was very young, he overheard adults discussing a terrible storm. The storm affected families and left their children without holiday presents. Santana offered to give his toys away as gifts for the children. He said that he could make more toys for himself out of paper. The name of his company today? PaperToy Clothing!

Santana's parents supported his creativity and decided to have some of his sketches printed on T-shirts. People who saw Santana's work wanted to know where they could purchase the T-shirts, and an online fashion business was born. He designs T-shirts for males from 10 to 25 years old, and he has created a 'wear and give' programme to give back to his community. For each T-shirt a customer buys, part of the sale price goes towards a programme to feed hungry children. 'I want to inspire boys and young men to action by producing wearable art that lives with you,' Santana says.

Teenage entrepreneur Maya Penn was only eight years old when she started her first business, Maya's Ideas. She makes eco-friendly clothing and accessories that are sold in many countries, including Australia, Canada, Denmark and Italy. When Maya was very young, her mother taught her to sew. Maya would find pieces of fabric around the house to turn into a scarf or hat. When she wore her creations in public, people would stop her and ask where they could buy them!

Even before she opened her business, Maya knew she wanted her clothes to reflect her beliefs. She decided that her items had to be eco-friendly and that she would donate 10 to 20 per cent of her profits to charities and environmental organisations. 'I've had a passion for protecting the environment and its creatures since I was little,' Maya says.

Maya Penn

VIDE⊙

1 BEFORE YOU WATCH **Discuss in pairs.**

1. Why do you think T-shirts are called T-shirts?

2. How many T-shirts have you got? Which one is your favourite? Why?

3. Why are T-shirts so popular all around the world?

2 **Read and circle.** You're going to watch *How Your T-shirt Can Make a Difference*. From the title, predict the purpose of the video. Circle the letter.

a. To sell you popular T-shirts

b. To show you how T-shirts are made

c. To help you make good choices

3 WHILE YOU WATCH **Listen and fill in an idea web. Watch scene 4.1.**

4 AFTER YOU WATCH **Work in pairs.** Number the order in which the information appears in the video.

_____ T-shirts use a lot of water and energy.

___1___ Cotton is everywhere.

_____ There is a solution. We can make a difference!

_____ We haven't got as much water on the planet as we think.

_____ Cotton has a major impact on the planet.

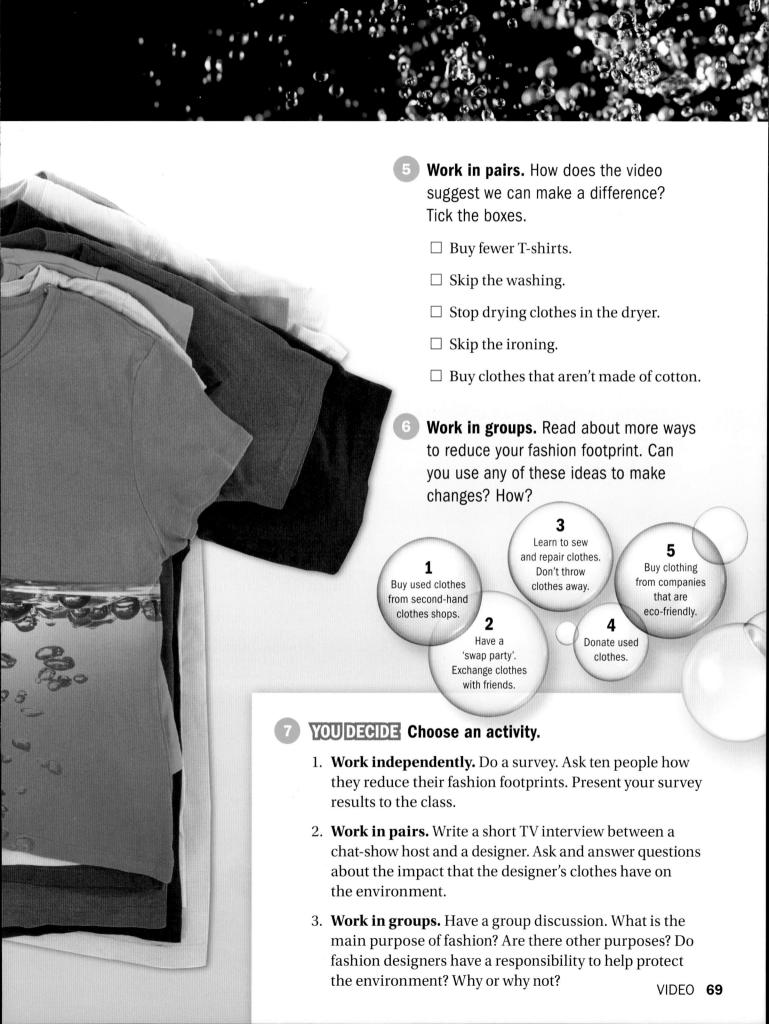

5 **Work in pairs.** How does the video suggest we can make a difference? Tick the boxes.

☐ Buy fewer T-shirts.

☐ Skip the washing.

☐ Stop drying clothes in the dryer.

☐ Skip the ironing.

☐ Buy clothes that aren't made of cotton.

6 **Work in groups.** Read about more ways to reduce your fashion footprint. Can you use any of these ideas to make changes? How?

1 Buy used clothes from second-hand clothes shops.

2 Have a 'swap party'. Exchange clothes with friends.

3 Learn to sew and repair clothes. Don't throw clothes away.

4 Donate used clothes.

5 Buy clothing from companies that are eco-friendly.

7 **YOU DECIDE** **Choose an activity.**

1. **Work independently.** Do a survey. Ask ten people how they reduce their fashion footprints. Present your survey results to the class.

2. **Work in pairs.** Write a short TV interview between a chat-show host and a designer. Ask and answer questions about the impact that the designer's clothes have on the environment.

3. **Work in groups.** Have a group discussion. What is the main purpose of fashion? Are there other purposes? Do fashion designers have a responsibility to help protect the environment? Why or why not?

GRAMMAR 056

Modals: Making suggestions and giving advice about present and past actions

You **shouldn't have bought** that leather jacket.

You **could have bought** that organic cotton jacket instead.

You **should be** more careful about reading labels.

You **could reduce** your footprint with a small change like this.

1 Read. Complete the dialogue with words from the list. Use *could*, *should*, *could have* or *should have*.

be	do	dry	hang	listen	put	wash	wear

Mum: You ___shouldn't have washed___ your new T-shirt. You just got it!

Pat: But I wore it to lunch with my friends and I spilt soup on it.

Mum: You _____ more careful. And instead of washing your T-shirt all by itself in the machine, you _____ it by hand in the sink. That way you save water.

Pat: What do you mean?

Mum: Did you know it takes 40 gallons of water to wash that T-shirt in the machine?

Pat: That much? I really _____ it in there.

Mum: And you _____ it in the dryer, either. It takes more than five times the energy to dry that T-shirt than it does to wash it. From now on, you _____ it on the clothes line so that the sun dries it – for free!

2 Work in pairs. Take turns thowing a coin (heads = 1 space; tails = 2 spaces). Make suggestions and give advice about present and past actions as instructed.

Go to page 161.

WRITING

In persuasive writing, we can support our point of view with facts and statistics. We use phrases such as:

_____ states that

according to _____

the facts show that _____

research shows that _____

1 **Read the model.** Work in pairs to identify the parts of the writing. How does the writer persuade the reader? Underline the phrases.

Have you ever seen someone wearing fur? Some people think fur is a fashion statement. Other people think it is more important to stop killing animals.

Research shows that millions of animals are killed for their fur each year. Some are hunted and trapped in the wild. Even more die at what are called fur-factory farms. According to groups that protect animals, most of the skins that people buy come from fur farms. On these farms, animals live in small, dirty cages until it's their turn to die.

People in the fur business say they help control animal populations. But the facts show that animals control their own populations. Fur factories also claim they do not have an impact on the environment, but that's not true, either. A real fur coat takes more than 20 times the energy needed to make a fake fur coat! The chemicals fur factories use also pollute the water.

Fashion lovers should know that every fur coat, jacket, waistcoat or hat represents animal suffering. This harm to animals and the environment will end only when people do their part and stop buying and wearing fur.

A mink

2 **Work in pairs.** Does the writing persuade you to do something about wearing fur? Why or why not?

3 **Write.** Persuade your readers to reduce their fashion footprint.

Make Good Choices

'I believe in a hands-on approach. Today we need everyone's involvement.'

Asher Jay
National Geographic Explorer, Creative Conservationist

1. **Watch scene 4.2.**

2. What are some things you can do by yourself or in your community to help protect animals used for fashion? To protect other animals?

3. What good choices can you make in your everyday life to protect the environment? Give at least three examples.

Make an Impact

YOU DECIDE Choose a project.

1 **Plan and write a blog entry about reducing one's fashion footprint.**

- Write the text.
- Collect photos and drawings.
- Share the blog and respond to questions and comments.

2 **Plan and hold an eco-friendly fashion show.**

- Collect donated and found materials.
- Use the materials to design clothing and accessories.
- Have a fashion show and film it.

3 **Plan and hold a Fashion Footprint Awareness Day.**

- Make posters and brochures.
- Conduct interviews in the community.
- Report on the day's activities for the school newspaper.

Express Yourself

The Garb Age

Fashion is about excess,
about wanting more.
It's indulgent, vain,
selfish to the core.

Excess is euphemism
for avoidable waste.
Buying without need
is in poor taste.

In a finite world
resources are scarce.
Surplus drains, and
Earth has no spares.

Fads repeat like history,
dated becomes news.
Reduce, repurpose, recycle.
Up-cycle and re-use!

Fight a failing model.
Save scraps, set the stage.
Sew your own designs,
but don't let your garb age.

2 **Work in groups.** Discuss the poem.

1. What do you think the poem is
   about? Circle the letter. Support
   your answer.

   a. buying trendy fashions
   b. reducing your fashion footprint
   c. buying only recycled clothing

2. The poem says we shouldn't buy
   things we don't need. Do you agree
   or disagree? Explain.

3 **Connect ideas.** In Unit 3, you learnt about group behaviours. In this unit, you learnt about fashion trends. What connection can you see between the two topics?

4 **YOU DECIDE** **Choose an activity.**

1. Choose a topic:
   • fashion and group behaviour
   • clothing and its impact on the environment

2. Choose a way to express yourself:
   • a poem or rap
   • a poster
   • a short video

3. Present your work.

Unit 1

Intonation in question tags

1 **Listen.** Notice how the voice goes up or down in the question tag. ∩ 114

He seems shy, doesn't he?

The voice goes down in the tag. In this case, the speaker is sure or almost sure.

You're not jealous, are you?

The voice goes up in the tag. In this case, the speaker is less sure.

2 **Listen and repeat.** Does the voice go up or down? Mark it with an arrow. Then circle the tags where the speaker is sure. ∩ 115

1. Your friends aren't very open-minded, are they?
2. Your sisters are very competitive, aren't they?
3. You didn't go to the party on Saturday, did you?
4. Your sister was at the party, wasn't she?
5. You were very self-conscious when you were younger, weren't you?
6. You've become more self-confident, haven't you?

3 **Work in pairs.** Listen and repeat each sentence. Then take turns repeating the question tags and answering them. ∩ 116

You love school, don't you? Yes, I do!

1. You love school, don't you? (sure)
2. English is easy, isn't it? (sure)
3. Your town has got a football team, hasn't it? (not sure)
4. Your family is big, isn't it? (not sure)
5. You haven't got a pet, have you? (sure)

Unit 2

Relaxed pronunciation: Modals + *have* + past participle

1 **Listen.** Notice how *have* is pronounced after modals. ∩ 117

They could have read about it.
He might have seen a jellyfish.
She must have been scared.

Have is often reduced. It sounds like the word *of.*

2 **Listen and repeat.** Make sure you reduce *have.* ∩ 118

1. She might have seen a spider.
2. They must have been afraid.
3. He could have read about the bear.
4. They could have been fire ants.
5. It might have been a rat.

3 **Work in pairs.** Take turns responding to the statements. Use *could / might / must* + *have* and the phrase in brackets. Reduce *have.*

Gina just screamed. She must have seen a cockroach.

1. A: Gina just screamed. (B: seen a cockroach)
2. A: Lee and Sue are afraid. (B: heard about the snakes)
3. A: Ray doesn't want to swim. (B: known about the sharks)
4. A: I was stung by a wasp! (B: been near its nest)
5. A: Julian went home. (B: felt sick)
6. A: Ann likes pit bulls. (B: read about them)

Unit 3

Pausing

1 **Listen.** Notice the short pauses between the groups of words that go together. 🎧 119

She's scared of wasps, / so we stayed in.

As a result, / we didn't go hiking.

In writing, pauses are often signalled by punctuation such as commas or full stops. But this is not always the case. Listen to this example. Notice the pause.

We stayed in / because he was scared.

Pausing will help your speech to be clear and easy to understand.

2 **Listen and repeat.** Draw a line where you hear a pause. 🎧 120

1. In my class, we often work in groups.
2. Students work hard, so they should get a break.
3. When I see a spider, I scream.
4. I don't like ants because they seem dirty.
5. I like elephants because they have complex emotions.

3 **Work in pairs.** Take turns completing the sentences using your own ideas. Add pauses when you speak. Your partner will respond. When you finish, swap roles.

> In my class, I ask a lot of questions.   Me, too!

1. In my class, _____ .
2. Students work hard, so they _____ .
3. When I see a spider, _____ .

Unit 4

Shouldn't have + past participle

1 **Listen.** Notice how *not have* is pronounced after *should*. 🎧 121

You shouldn't have thrown it away.
I shouldn't have washed it.

Not have or the contracted *n't* is often reduced to sound like *unt*. *Have* sounds like the word *of*. There is just a small difference between the negative and positive forms. Listen closely.

He should have bought it.
He shouldn't have bought it.

2 **Listen.** Circle the form you hear. Then listen again and repeat. 🎧 122

1. A: Oh, I (should / shouldn't) have bought this shirt.
   B: You (should / shouldn't) have cut the tags off. Now you can't return it!

2. A: You (should / shouldn't) have gone to that shop. You (should / shouldn't) have tried the new one I told you about.
   B: Oh, I forgot! You (should / shouldn't) have reminded me.

3 **Work in pairs.** Take turns practising the conversations with your partner. Use *shouldn't have* and the words in brackets.

1. A: I'm so tired today! (B: gone to bed so late)
2. A: I ruined my jeans! (B: washed them in hot water)
3. A: I failed the test! (B: missed so many lessons)
4. A: He made me late! (B: waited for him)

> I'm so tired today!   You shouldn't have gone to bed so late.

Irregular Verbs

Infinitive	Past simple	Past participle	Infinitive	Past simple	Past participle
be	were	been	leave	left	left
beat	beat	beaten	lend	lent	lent
become	became	become	let	let	let
begin	began	begun	lie (down)	lay	lain
bend	bent	bent	light	lit	lit
bet	bet	bet	lose	lost	lost
bite	bit	bitten	make	made	made
bleed	bled	bled	mean	meant	meant
blow	blew	blown	meet	met	met
break	broke	broken	overcome	overcame	overcome
bring	brought	brought	pay	paid	paid
build	built	built	put	put	put
burn	burnt	burnt	quit	quit	quit
buy	bought	bought	read	read	read
carry	carried	carried	ride	rode	ridden
catch	caught	caught	ring	rang	rung
choose	chose	chosen	rise	rose	risen
come	came	come	run	ran	run
cost	cost	cost	say	said	said
cut	cut	cut	see	saw	seen
deal	dealt	dealt	sell	sold	sold
dig	dug	dug	send	sent	sent
dive	dived	dived	set	set	set
do	did	done	sew	sewed	sewn
draw	drew	drawn	shake	shook	shaken
dream	dreamt	dreamt	shine	shone	shone
drink	drank	drunk	show	showed	shown
drive	drove	driven	shrink	shrank	shrunk
dry	dried	dried	shut	shut	shut
eat	ate	eaten	sing	sang	sung
fall	fell	fallen	sink	sank	sunk
feed	fed	fed	sit	sat	sat
feel	felt	felt	sleep	slept	slept
fight	fought	fought	slide	slid	slid
find	found	found	speak	spoke	spoken
flee	fled	fled	spend	spent	spent
fly	flew	flown	spin	spun	spun
forbid	forbade	forbidden	stand	stood	stood
forget	forgot	forgotten	steal	stole	stolen
forgive	forgave	forgiven	stick	stuck	stuck
freeze	froze	frozen	sting	stung	stung
fry	fried	fried	stink	stank	stunk
get	got	got	strike	struck	struck
give	gave	given	swear	swore	sworn
go	went	gone	sweep	swept	swept
grind	ground	ground	swim	swam	swum
grow	grew	grown	swing	swung	swung
hang	hung	hung	take	took	taken
have	had	had	teach	taught	taught
hear	heard	heard	tear	tore	torn
hide	hid	hidden	tell	told	told
hit	hit	hit	think	thought	thought
hold	held	held	throw	threw	thrown
hurt	hurt	hurt	understand	understood	understood
keep	kept	kept	wake	woke	woken
kneel	knelt	knelt	wear	wore	worn
knit	knitted	knitted	weave	wove	woven
know	knew	known	win	won	won
lay	laid	laid	write	wrote	written
lead	led	led			

Two-word verbs – Inseparable

Verb	Meaning	Sample sentence
amount to	be the same as; turn out to be	The total **amounts to** five hundred. Some people thought he would not **amount to** anything, but he became famous.
apply for	to make a request	Do you plan to **apply for** a summer job?
apply to	be relevant	The rules **apply to** everyone!
ask around	ask several people	I'll **ask around** in case anyone found a lost phone.
break down	stop functioning	The car **broke down** yesterday.
break up	end a relationship	Did you hear that Lara and Renato **broke up**?
calm down	relax after being angry	**Calm down**! Everything will be OK.
check in	register at a hotel or airport	We can't **check in** until one o'clock.
check out	leave a hotel	He **checked out** at 10.20 and went straight to the airport.
cheer up	become happier	**Cheer up**! I'm sure your team will do better next time.
come across	find unexpectedly	I **came across** a very interesting article about crocodiles.
come from	originate in	Mangoes originally **come from** Asia.
count on	rely on	Please be there on time. I'm **counting on** you!
dress up	wear nice clothes	Mum, do I really need to **dress up** for the party?
eat out	eat at a restaurant	Why don't we **eat out** on Friday?
end up	eventually do/decide	We **ended up** going to the cinema last night.
engage in	take part in	The head teacher **engaged in** talks with the student council.
fall apart	break into pieces	Mum, I need a new desk. This one's **falling apart**.
fall down	fall to the ground	The vase **fell down** and smashed.
find out	learn	I was so excited when I **found out** we were going to Spain!
fit in	blend in; belong because you're similar	Teenagers wear certain clothes to **fit in**.
get along	be friendly with someone	I really like Tom. We **get along** well.
get over	recover from a problem	I know she's upset you didn't call her, but she'll **get over** it.
get together	meet; gather	Let's **get together** on Wednesday after school!
get up	get out of bed; rise	I **get up** at seven o'clock every day.
give in	surrender; quit	I won't **give in** to pressure from my friends.
give up	stop trying	This puzzle is really hard, but we won't **give up**!
go ahead	do; begin to do	Why don't you **go ahead** and invite her to the party?
go back	return	He **went back** to the site and discovered a second dinosaur.
go over	review	Let's **go over** the presentation before the lesson.
grow up	become an adult	I **grew up** in China.
hang in	stay positive	**Hang in** there. I'm sure you'll find the phone.
hang on	wait	**Hang on** a minute. I'm on the phone.
hang out	spend time	Do you want to **hang out** on Saturday?
hold on	wait	**Hold on** a second! I think I found the answer.
lead to	cause to happen	His research **led to** the discovery of a new species.

Verb	Meaning	Sample sentence
light up	become bright	The sky **lit up** with fireworks.
log in/on	sign in to a website or app	I can't **log in** because I can't remember my password.
look after	take care of	I have to **look after** my little sister on Sunday.
look back	think about things that happened in the past	**Looking back**, I think the other project topic was more interesting.
look for	try to find	What are you **looking for**? Did you lose something?
look into	try to find out about	I need to **look into** it. I'll let you know tomorrow.
not care for	not like	I do**n't** really **care for** opera.
pass away	die	I heard Kim's grandma **passed away**.
prey on	hunt and kill for food	Do lions **prey on** zebras?
rave about	talk or write very enthusiastically	Critics are **raving about** the new film.
rely on	trust; depend on	Do you think we **rely on** technology too much?
run away	escape; leave	Our dog **ran away**!
run into	meet unexpectedly; collide	Yesterday I **ran into** my old teacher. I **ran into** a tree.
stand out	be noticeable	I was the only one wearing purple. I really **stood out**.
take off	start to fly	The flight **took off** on time.
turn out	result; happen	I thought everyone in my family had a mobile phone. It **turns out** my uncle refuses to get one!
wake up	stop sleeping	I usually **wake up** at six o'clock.
warm up	prepare for exercise	Do you **warm up** before football games?
work out	be successful; exercise	Everyone liked our presentation. It **worked out** well! I prefer to **work out** in the gym when it's cold.

Two-word verbs – Separable

Verb	Meaning	Sample sentence
back up	support	His friends **backed** him **up**.
call off	cancel	They had planned a party, but they had to **call** it **off**.
calm down	help relax	Let's play soft music to **calm** the baby **down**.
carry out	do or complete something	They are **carrying out** research on ancient birds.
check out	observe; notice	**Check out** my new phone!
cheer up	try to make someone happy	Why don't we get some flowers to **cheer** her **up**?
clean up	organise; clean	Can you **clean** that **up**? Guests are arriving soon.
cut down	make something fall to the ground	They're **cutting down** too many trees.
cut off	remove by cutting	Did you read about that hiker that had to **cut off** his own arm?
draw in	capture the interest	This book really **drew** me **in**.
equip with	supply with	They **equipped** the astronauts **with** extra oxygen tanks.
fill out/in	write information in a form	Remember to **fill out** the form before the end of the week. **Fill in** your details on page 6.

Verb	Meaning	Sample sentence
fill up	fill to the top	Don't **fill up** the cup. I need room for milk.
find out	discover information	How did you **find** that **out**?
get across	make understandable	We need to add more examples to **get** the idea **across**!
give back	return something	Have you still got my book? Can you **give** it **back** to me?
give up	stop (a habit)	I'm **giving up** coffee!
hand in	submit	Did you **hand in** your homework on time?
hand out	distribute	I'll make copies and **hand** them **out**.
let down	disappoint	I really want you to come to the party. Don't **let** me **down**.
let in	allow to come in	They didn't **let** him **in** with his rucksack.
light up	make bright	At night the stars **light** the sky **up**.
look up	find information	Can you **look** it **up** in a dictionary?
make up	lie about; invent	That can't be true. I think he **made** it **up**.
mix up	confuse things or people	They always **mix** me **up** with my sister.
put off	postpone	Can we **put off** the meeting until next week?
put together	assemble	Can you help me **put** this **together**?
take down	remove	They **took down** the painting because it was controversial.
take off	remove	**Take off** that coat. You'll be too hot.
take over	gain control of	He **took over** the company when his father died.
throw away	put in the rubbish; get rid of	Don't **throw away** plastic bottles. Recycle them.
track down	find after a long search	I'm trying to **track down** a friend from my childhood.
try on	put on to see if it fits	I **tried on** my sister's shoes, but they didn't fit.
turn away	reject; refuse to admit	Hundreds of people were **turned away** from the audition.
turn down	decrease the strength	**Turn** the TV **down** a bit. It's too loud.
turn off	power off	Don't forget to **turn off** the lights when you leave.
turn on	power on	**Turn on** the TV. The match has started!
turn up	increase the strength	I can't hear. Can you **turn up** the volume?
warm up	make warmer	Can you **warm up** the milk?
work out	find a solution	I'm sure you'll **work** it **out**.

Three-word verbs – Inseparable

Verb	Meaning	Sample sentence
add up to	become a certain amount; result in something	The total **adds up to** two hundred.
break up with	end a relationship	She **broke up with** her boyfriend last week.
come down with	become ill	He **came down with** a cold.
come up against	face; confront	He **came up against** many obstacles during his research.
come up with	think of; find a solution	She **came up with** an excellent plan.
cut down on	use less of; do less	You should **cut down on** your screen time!
get along with	be friendly with	My sister **gets along with** everyone!
get round to	find time to finally do	I finally **got round to** writing my blog.
get away with	not get caught	How did you **get away with** not doing your homework?
get back into	become interested again	I stopped playing football two years ago, but then I **got back into** it.

Verb	Meaning	Sample sentence
get out of	avoid doing something you don't want to do	I think that's just an excuse to **get out of** doing the project!
give up on	lose hope that somebody or something will succeed	I **gave up on** trying to become an athlete.
grow out of	change your mind over time; become too big for	He wants to be a rock star, but I'm sure he'll **grow out of** it. You'll **grow out of** that jacket before winter is over!
look down on	feel that somebody is less important	Many people **looked down on** him and his art, but he went on to become a famous artist.
look forward to	be excited about (something in the future)	I **look forward to** going on holiday.
look out for	protect; take care of	He's very selfish! He only **looks out for** himself.
look up to	have a lot of respect for	Many youngsters **look up to** athletes or pop stars.
play around with	try several options	I **played around with** it until I found the problem!
put up with	tolerate	Our teacher doesn't **put up with** bad behaviour.
run out of	use everything	I think we've **run out of** milk. Can you get some?
stand up for	defend	Don't let him make fun of you. **Stand up for** yourself!
watch out for	be alert; anticipate	**Watch out for** deer crossing the road!

Verbs followed by infinitives and gerunds

Verbs followed by infinitive

He **agreed to go**.

afford	deserve	offer
agree	fail	plan
appear	happen	pretend
arrange	hesitate	refuse
attempt	hope	seem
care	intend	tend
claim	learn	vow
decide	manage	wait
demand		

Verbs followed by infinitive or noun/pronoun + infinitive

He **wants to learn** French.
I **want him to learn** French.

ask	prepare
choose	promise
dare	want
expect	wish
need	would like

Verbs followed by noun/pronoun + infinitive

I **convinced her to try** sushi.

cause	motivate
challenge	order
convince	persuade
empower	remind
forbid	tell
force	urge
hire	warn
invite	

Verbs followed by gerund or noun/pronoun + infinitive

They don't **allow surfing** here.
They didn't **allow him to surf** here.

advise
allow
encourage
permit
require

Verbs followed by a gerund

You should **avoid swimming** there.

admit	delay	imagine	mind	report
anticipate	deny	involve	miss	resist
appreciate	discuss	justify	postpone	risk
avoid	dislike	keep	practise	suggest
can't help	enjoy	look forward to	put off	understand
carry on	feel like	mention	recommend	
consider	finish			

Verbs followed by infinitive or gerund (similar meaning)

I **hate waking** up early.
I **hate to wake** up early.

begin	hate	prefer
can't bear	like	propose
can't stand	love	start
continue		

Verbs followed by infinitive or gerund (different meaning)

I **remember going** there last year.
I **remembered to go** to the shop.

forget	remember
go on	stop
quit	try
regret	

Start

Compare

Contrast
two of your
teachers.

You're lucky!
Move ahead
2 spaces.

Compare

Contrast
two favourite
TV characters.

You're stubborn!
Move back
1 space.

Compare
yourself and your
best friend.

Contrast

You're energetic!
Move ahead
2 spaces.

Congratulations!
You've finished!

Compare
yourself and
a brother, sister
or cousin.

Contrast

End

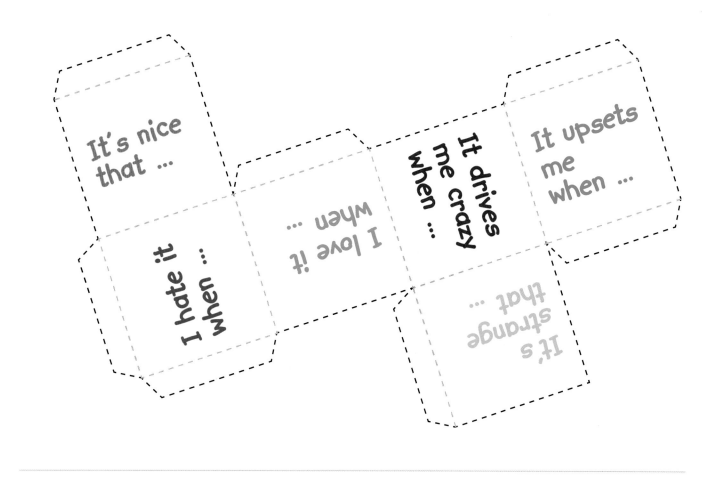

Unit 4 Cutouts Use with Activity 3 on page 63.

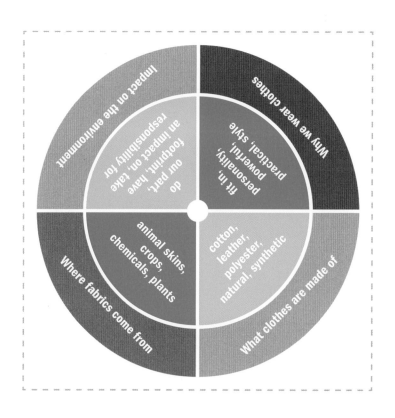

true

Giraffes clean their ears with their tongues.

true

Sharks grow around 30,000 teeth in their lifetime.

false

Camels don't sweat, so their humps are full of water.

true

Rats clean themselves frequently. They even wash their faces with water.

true

Kangaroos can't walk backwards.

true

A bird called the Egyptian plover goes inside a crocodile's mouth to clean its teeth and then flies out safely.

true

Crocodiles can't stick out their tongues.

false

Hippos sweat a red-pink version of blood.

false

Polar bears cover their black noses with a paw when they want to hide in the snow.

true

Some octopuses can be poisonous.

true

The mantis shrimp has a special front arm that can heat surrounding water up to 4,700°C (8,500°F).

true

The giant Goliath bird-eater spider can cover the head of a man.

Start

Make a sentence about army ants.

Use: **Because of**

You're lucky!

Move forward 3 spaces.

Make a sentence about schools of fish and predators.

Use: **As a result**

End

Make a sentence about cockroaches.

Use: **So**

Make a sentence about elephant group behaviour.

Use: **Since**

Make a sentence about yourself and a friend.

Use: **So**

You're unlucky!

Move back 1 space.

Make a sentence about yourself and a family member.

Use: **Since**

You're unlucky!

Move back 1 space.

Make a sentence about bees and wasps.

Use: **Consequently**

Make a sentence about yourself.

Use: **Because**

Make a sentence about monkeys.

Use: **Because of**

Make a sentence about yourself.

Use: **As a result**

Make a sentence about groups of birds flying together.

Use: **Due to**

Make a sentence about mosquitoes.

Use: **Due to**

You're unlucky!

Move back 1 space.

159

START

Your friend bought another pair of trainers – for a total of €25.

Your little brother always takes your favourite hat without asking.

You have a small fashion footprint! **Advance 2 spaces.**

Your sister washed your favourite white dress with a load of black clothes.

Your friend borrowed your new jeans without asking.

Your brother got chocolate ice cream all over your favourite shirt.

You don't think before you buy! **Go back 2 spaces.**

Your dad throws out old ties he doesn't wear any more.

You do your part to protect the planet. **Advance 2 spaces.**

Your aunt isn't interested in reducing her fashion footprint.

You don't recycle old clothing! **Go back 2 spaces.**

A classmate forgot to collect clothes for the recycling party.

FINISH